Sufficient Grace

By Kelly Gerken

Comfort PUBLISHING

Sufficient Grace

For information, address Comfort Publishing, 296 Church St. N., Concord, NC 28025. The views expressed in this book are not necessarily those of the publisher.

First printing

Book cover design by Marcy Shultz
Cover photograph by Rachel Sharpe

ISBN: 978-1-938388-47-7
Published by Comfort Publishing, LLC
www.comfortpublishing.com

Printed in the United States of America

Acknowledgements

It took me close to ten years to write this book. A lot can happen in ten years. I don't even know how to begin to thank the people who have walked with me and my family through the trials of loss and grief, through seasons of joy, and many who walk with me now, as we serve grieving families.

How does one find adequate words for gratefulness of this magnitude?

Thank you ... first, and forever ... to the God whose grace is always enough and never runs out.

Thank you to my husband ... who stayed, and who loves me better than anyone ever could. And to our children ... those who call me mom and those who dance in heaven. I spent many late nights distracted, writing. I spend many late nights still, ministering to bereaved families. My family has heard me tell the story on these pages, countless times to countless audiences. I will keep the telling the story, as long as I have breath and an ear to listen. They didn't ask to be on this journey, any more than I did. But, they go, willingly ... to light lanterns at remembrance ceremonies, to stuff Comfort Bears, to churches and events to listen to a story they lived ... to listen to me speak of the hardest moments of our lives. They honor God, and they honor me.

And, the ones dancing in heaven ... they have taught me more lessons about grace and faith than anyone on planet earth. They continue to teach me and thousands of others ... because they lived.

Thank you, to Dinah ... the woman who taught me how to be married, how to honor both my husband and my God.

Thank you, to my mother ... who taught me how to make lemonade from the lemons in this life.

Thank you, to Ginny ... my fierce friend, who sat beside me through every agonizing inch of that wilderness walk, the only other woman (aside from medical staff) who held our Thomas Patrick in her arms.

Thank you to my father ... who recently gave me the greatest gift any dad can give to his daughter or son. He told me he is proud of me and the work I do, that he admires me for being brave enough to do it. He said to never change who I am or how I write, even if others don't get it. There is great power in being told that who you are, the person God created you to be ... is good enough, just right ... beautiful, even. No matter old we are, that really sums up all we long to hear from our dads.

We are surrounded by beautiful friends, whose kindness and love are more than can be mentioned in the pages of this book. I'm thankful for each of them, for our church family at Harvest Fellowship, for the women who've gathered around my kitchen table, praying prayers.

Thank you to my prayer warrior friend, Lynette, who first said this story needed to be written. And, to Betsy, who handed it back to me years ago after my first 67 page draft, stating, "A lot has to happen before this is a book." She was right.

Thank you, to the group of my son's friends I've come to lovingly refer to as the "boys in my kitchen", children who've been adopted into my heart. The ones who've listened to my stories, eaten at my dinner table, offered hugs after a long night at the hospital supporting a family, stuffed Comfort Bears, and gone on to speak of babies with brief lives on college campuses with the courage few young men know ... the courage to show compassion. Those are the men who will change their corner of the world. They've changed mine.

Thank you to everyone who serves as the hands and feet of Jesus, pouring love into every offering at Sufficient Grace Ministries, to my dear friend and partner in ministry, Holly Haas, to our tiny but mighty board of directors, and every volunteer on the SGM team.

Thank you to the mothers and families we have the privilege of walking alongside through the wilderness of grief, for allowing us to stand with you again and again in the place where heaven meets earth, for the sacred and incredible gift of honoring every precious life, no matter how brief. You have taught me much about what love looks like.

Thank you to Rachel Sharpe for using her beautiful gift of photography to capture our book cover, and for the patience and vision to get it "just right". Your heart in capturing the beauty of birth and babies of all gestational ages, honoring each precious life, astounds me.

Thank you to everyone at Comfort Publishing, for working with me with such grace, for understanding how deeply personal every piece of this story is to me, and for being willing to take these words from the depths of my heart, and put them in print.

Two foolish young teenagers entered this world unplanned and grew up unsure of their purpose. They were lonely with little understanding of the love they craved so much. It seemed they were destined for disaster, or at least to repeat the mistakes of the generations that came before them. But God had other plans for these two …

… God chose the foolish things of the world to shame the wise;
God chose the weak things of the world to shame the strong.
He chose the lowly things of this world and the despised things —
and the things that are not — to nullify the things that are,
so that no one may boast before Him.
– I Corinthians 1: 27-29

Chapter One
A Cord of Three Strands

Like two sparrows in a hurricane, trying to find their way;
With a head full of dreams and faith that
could move anything;
They've heard it's all uphill, but all they know is how they feel;
The world says they'll never make it … love says they will …
– from the song, Sparrows in a Hurricane *by Marc Alan*
Springer and performed by Tanya Tucker

If it had been a movie, the music would have swelled romantically and the camera would have moved in for a close-up, capturing the twinkle in my eyes and framing our faces as we danced across the floor at a friend's wedding. With one whisper, he caused me to throw my head back and laugh with my entire, noticeably pregnant body. The dramatic movie effects would indicate that this moment was significant in defining the lives and the story of these young lovers.

In reality, I felt pretty in my third-hand, black-covered-with-pastel-pink-and-blue-flowers maternity skirt and top ensemble. And I felt loved in the arms of my young husband. After our dance, I went to refuel with a glass of 7-UP, and an acquaintance commented wistfully how happy and in love Tim and I looked. We were twenty-one years old, married for a little over two years, and expecting for the second time - twins, no less. It was a snapshot from a time when we were still innocent and invincible.

Three years before, while Tim was just a senior in high school, we fittingly played Tanya Tucker's, "Sparrows in a Hurricane", for our wedding dance. We were eighteen years old. He made me laugh during that song, too. Only that time, he was making fun of the fact that we were dancing to this sappy song in his aunt's basement for our down-home reception in front of our family and high school/college- aged friends. I didn't feel nearly as pretty that night in my cream-colored pantsuit, with a baby boy to nurse.

The first year of our marriage, Tim and I lived in a one-bedroom apartment with our son, Timothy. Tim went to high school and worked full time, first at a car wash; then at a metal spinning shop. I worked as a waitress at night, and he took care of our son while I worked. My mom helped out, watching Timothy while our shifts overlapped. Tim was the first person allowed to go to high school part time in our district. He had to request special permission from the school board to work part of the day, and some of his teachers spoke up on his behalf.

One teacher reassured my mother during this tumultuous time, "Tim and Kelly are no fly-by-night couple. I think they can make it."

I don't know if he remembers saying it, or if he ever knew that his words got back to us, but I clung to those words. Knowing that someone placed at least a small amount of confidence in us made us feel determined and encouraged.

I knew so little about life and love. We were very young. Overnight it seemed I had become a wife and mother; I was the adult now. And as much as I couldn't wait to grow up and get out of my mother's house, I felt myself longing for the feeling of being taken care of by my mother, or someone … anyone. I had terrible nightmares almost every night. Depressed and lonelier than I had ever felt, I was in charge. If there was a need, I had to meet it. If there was an emergency, I would have to take care of it.

Tim, overwhelmed with the sudden weight of adult burdens thrust completely on his young shoulders grew grouchy and distant. We never talked, it seemed, and the laughter that had once stolen my heart, all but disappeared. I was so lost in my own pain and disappointment; I couldn't see Tim's struggles. Instead, feeling overburdened, unloved, and alone, I placed more emotional demands on him. It was a vicious cycle that drove a wedge between us.

Inexperienced in healthy relationships, I didn't realize then how much he had sacrificed to take care of us. He spent his senior year working in a machine shop. We didn't go to prom, and his baby and wife sat in the bleachers among the audience at his graduation. Youth disappeared for him. Yet, he never uttered a word of complaint or protest. I thought I wanted so much from him. I had no idea in my teenage, self-absorbed mind that he had laid down his very life for me and our child. He was already beginning to display what it looks like to love another human being much better than I was able to give him in return. I didn't see all of that then. I didn't know just how young eighteen looked, until many years later, when looking into our son Timothy's eighteen year old, dark brown eyes. I only saw my own ache for more, and my own desperate struggle to navigate this unknown grown-up world.

Our son Timothy was the one ray of hope in those early years, the silver lining shining through the dark clouds. He was the glue holding us together. We wanted a better life for him, the cry of every parent's heart. We never wanted our children to know the devastating effects of divorce. But, if something didn't change between us, we were bound to repeat the pattern of the generations before us.

Just when it looked like we were about to be swallowed up in our own failures, a childhood friend visited me. She said she had recently "accepted Jesus as her Savior."

Hmmm. Jesus, I remember Him … vaguely, I thought. I reminisced about walking to Sunday School on crisp, autumn mornings with a song in my heart, the magic of walking out of the Christmas Eve service and catching the big flaky snowflakes on my tongue, the eager desire to spread the gospel as a missionary one day churning in my heart while I sat in Catechism as a middle school student, and the desperate, guilt-ridden prayers I prayed during my rebellious teen years while clinging to my bible in the dark.

Oh, but I couldn't possibly go to Him now after the mess I've made of everything. After all, He's perfect. I couldn't let Him see me like this. There's no way He could forgive the things I've done and the person I've become, but it was nice for my friend Ginny.

Over the next few weeks, I saw Ginny often. She would come to sit with me and listen when I was feeling extra low. At the time, I didn't realize it, but I was in a very deep depression. It was even affecting me physically. I was exhausted and experiencing stomach problems. Ginny would come and help me with the house. She didn't speak about Jesus, much. She showed Him to me with her kindness and her love.

Slowly, I began to consider the Jesus that I once knew. He was the One who comforted me when I was alone and afraid as a child. He was the One I prayed to as a young girl. His was the

Word I studied as an adolescent and clung to when fear would grip me in the dark of night. He was in the place I walked to on Sunday mornings, the place filled with love and acceptance. Could it be? Could that place of acceptance exist still? *Maybe, but not for me. I had done too much. No, I would have to find a way through on my own.*

It was my mess, and I would have to clean it up. I tried for awhile. But I failed miserably. How could I fail at this? The goal of my heart from the time I was a little girl was to never let my children down. I would get it right. Our children would not suffer. They would grow up with both their mom and dad. Love would prevail. *I promised myself, so it had to be true. Love had to be enough, right?* But the limited view of love I held in my young teenage mind was not enough.

What can I do? There's no way out. I can't even fix this. I'm so alone, I thought feeling more lost, hopeless, and rejected than ever.

At the end of my rope, I threw myself unto our hand-me-down bed, crying sobs of despair. Once I had cried enough that my head ached even more than my heart, I looked over at Timothy giggling and cooing carelessly in his crib. All of a sudden, it was clear. There was one thing bigger than ME and all of my feelings. This little person needed me. He needed me to be his mom, the grown-up, the safe place, and the one who loved him more than she loved herself. (*Greater love has no one than this, that he lay down his life for his friends.* – John 15:13) I felt so weak and broken. I couldn't fight anymore. I wept on the floor of our room. This time, my weeping was not in self-pity … but finally, surrender.

As he bounced gleefully in his crib, I knelt to my knees and asked God to help me, confessing my sin and my great need for Jesus. I needed to be rescued as much as anyone can need rescuing. I couldn't do it on my own. Lost, alone, and afraid, I asked Him to take my life and to be my Lord. And when I stood up, I was a new creation.

Therefore, if anyone is in Christ, he is a new creation;
the old is gone, the new has come!
– 2 Corinthians 5:17

I didn't completely realize it yet, but this marriage had welcomed a third party. We weren't able to save each other. So that night, I asked the only One I knew who was big enough to save us both — to save us all.

Two are better than one, because they have a good return
for their work: If one falls down, his friend can help him up.
But pity the man who falls and has no one to help him up!
Also, if two lie down together, they will keep warm. But how can
one keep warm alone?
Though one may be overpowered, two can defend themselves.
A cord of three strands is not quickly broken.
– Ecclesiastes 4:9-12

Eleven-month-old Timothy and I began attending a new church with Ginny and her family. It was January 1, 1995. When I entered the service, they were singing the words, "As the deer panteth for the water … so my soul longeth after thee. You alone are my heart's desire … And I long to worship thee." My spirit immediately stirred, and I let the refreshing beauty of the words wash over me, as I worshipped at His feet. Finally, I was getting the truth. I became immersed in God's Word, thirsty for knowledge of Him. I went to church twice a week, living from Wednesday to Sunday. Suddenly, my starving soul was getting fed food that would nourish, strengthen, and sustain.

Amidst all the lies of this world, there was something that could hold true. Finally, after all the people whose love grows cold, all the broken hearts and people that walked away, there was a love that would never fail. I learned that I was not unlovable. I learned that I was worthy because the blood of Jesus had washed me clean and made me new. My sins could be forgiven. There was hope in Him. The God of the Universe wanted to be my Father. I could look back over my life and see that He had always been with me, leading me gently to come to know Him as my Lord and Savior. He had kept me and prepared me, and I had never been alone.

When I was eight years old and stood on the porch, watching my father drive away after I spoke words that you can't take back …

When, at age twelve, I held my brothers close to keep them from watching another father walk away, feeling the numbness wash over me, covering the hurts that run too deep to fully feel …

When I floundered through my teenage years, soaking in the attention I craved whether on the stage or on the back of some boy's motorcycle, numbing the persistent hurts with various distractions, pushing my mother away with my ugly words and rebellion …

In all of it, He never left me alone.

I have this thing about being alone, or being left by those I love. My abandonment issues became abundantly clear a couple years ago at a Women of Faith conference, when among thousands of women, I sobbed like a baby as Marilyn Meberg spoke about her book, *Love Me, Never Leave Me.* I stink at goodbyes quite profoundly, actually, and do my best to avoid the loathsome inevitability at all costs.

Last summer I blogged about a book by Karen Kingsbury that shares this sentiment well. The excerpt from the book, *Leaving,* shown below, is from a Pastor's sermon:

"Goodbyes were one of the hardest things about life … one way or another people were always leaving. Always moving on … Life changes. People come and go, and seasons never last."

*"Nothing stays the same. We can count on that. Good times come and go … finances are ever changing … our health will eventually fail us. **And through death or decision, everyone we know will someday leave us.**"*

*"All except for Jesus Christ. Jesus will never leave you nor forsake you. And because of that we have strength to love with all our hearts … even unaware of what tomorrow brings. That's what I want you to take away from today's service. **Jesus stays.**"*
— *Leaving, Chapter One:* by Karen Kingsbury

The revelation that Jesus would never leave me cut to the very heart of my broken places, whispering a promise. Hope was born, where desperation once lived.

With great enthusiasm, I delved into learning about Jesus, and His Word changed me. I was forsaking some of my old party-girl ways. Tim wasn't sure what to think about my newfound enthusiasm, and the drastic changes in me. Sometimes it was a source of contention between us. I can see how it would be a shock to think he fell for the girl who could drink as much as the boys, the one dancing on a table by the end of the night. How could the girl he married, the one poring over her bible and singing in church be the same girl he fell in love with?

> *... since you have taken off your old self with its practices*
> *and have put on the new self, which is being renewed in*
> *knowledge in the image of its Creator.*
> *— Colossians 3:9b &10*

Ginny was a great friend to me, along with many other wise women at the church, (Dinah, Betsy, Becki and others) who gently and lovingly listened to my desperate longings to have the marriage God intended for me. (In my opinion, that would be a marriage that fulfilled all my wants and desires! Boy, did I have a lot to learn.). They taught me what being a wife meant, both by their example as godly wives and by referring me to the Scriptures. They truly exemplified the women in Titus 2. And I became an eager student. I read my Bible as well as every Christian book written on marriage that I could get my hands on. If it weren't for their obedience to God's leading and diligence to follow Him in their marriage, I would hate to think what could have happened to my precious family.

My friend Dinah was an eccentric and fabulous woman. She counteracted the ideas that shaped and molded most of the philosophies I acquired about life and marriage growing up in a household where husbands leave and women ruled the roost.

From The Sufficient Grace Blog:

Here are some of my favorite Dinah-isms. I have a whole-lifetime of her words in my heart.

On marriage and keeping a home ...

"You're giving that man way too many words. He cannot handle every thought in your mind and every feeling you have. Without a word ... He is won without a word. How do you not know that after growing up with all those brothers?"

Incidentally ... she also said the above phrase about my boys ... whenever I gave them too many directions or over explained ... She would say, "You know he heard about three words of what you just said, don't you?"

"Your home should be a haven to all who enter."

"Let the kids play, but start getting things in order an hour before your husband comes home: have the house picked up, children clean and presentable, supper cooked and comb your hair, put on some lipstick, and wear something pretty before that man comes home. He should come home to order and peace."

"My mother took a nap every day. I think that's a good idea."

"If it blesses your husband when you make him breakfast before work, then get up and make him breakfast."

"The way you present yourselves and your family is a reflection of whether or not you honor your husband."

"Never get too tired, angry, hungry, or lonely."

"Make sure those boys know how to conduct themselves in any situation. You never know when you might have to eat dinner with the president."

"Make sure those boys know how to treat a lady with respect and use their manners."

"Make sure those boys know the Word. Better to pay them to learn scripture than to do their chores or get good grades. Sometimes good, godly fear and reverence are necessary for a boy to know. They need to respect the things of God. Respect is the language young men speak. Then, they can learn about grace."

And, one of my personal favorites:

"If your husband comes home from a long day of work and promptly falls asleep on the couch, be grateful he's sleeping on your couch, as opposed to the couch in someone else's house. And, be grateful he loves your family enough to work so hard that he is tired enough to fall asleep on the couch."

She truly was a master in the art of honoring husbands; probably, because she learned from the best. Her mother, Ruth, was adept in the art of honoring and loving a husband. She passed down quite a legacy to Dinah, and Dinah to her daughters, and to me.

As I reflect on those early years, it is evident I didn't realize the great sacrifices Tim made for our family at such a tender age. He just did the next thing before him. I admire and respect him more than most men I've met, for his ability to always pull up his bootstraps, cowboy up, and do what needs to be done. We need more men on this earth with such integrity and conviction.

The amazing thing, in those tender years, is that while I longed for God to change Tim's heart, it was me that He began to change. He showed me that I needed to lay down my life and my selfishness and show Tim love – not the kind of love I thought, but a love without conditions. That love is only possible with the help of the Holy Spirit. This love is perfect and it comes from God. We are unable to love others completely, perfectly and unconditionally on our own. This was not the answer that I had in mind, but God wasn't finished with me yet. God did provide. He always does provide for us, sustain us and grow us. For His grace is sufficient for us … no matter what we face.

Chapter Two
The Pruning Begins

When Timothy was two years old, I was expecting again. Tim and I went to the doctor appointment for my first ultrasound, filled with nervous anticipation. The obstetrician kept saying "hmmm," which didn't help matters.

"What's wrong?" I asked, shaking.

He said, "Well, it looks like we have two babies here!"

"What?! Two Babies! Are they O.K.? What?! Two? How can we do this? Aren't there more complications with twins? Oh my goodness!" I cried as the tears poured down my cheeks.

I was scared and excited, but mostly scared. It was very overwhelming. Apparently there was more than one thing that I hadn't quite learned to trust God with yet.

Tim was a little beside himself as well. I held my sobs in until I was safely behind the curtain where we ladies go to change from the paper dress to our more discreet, and much less drafty "regular" clothes. I didn't want Tim to know how afraid I suddenly felt.

He shook the curtain. "What's wrong? Are you alright? Aren't you happy?" he asked when I didn't come out right away.

"Yes … it's just a lot to process. Twin pregnancies sometimes have problems. I'm just a little overwhelmed, I guess. This was unexpected," I replied, doing my best to steady my voice.

"It will all be O.K.," he said, and emphasized his effort to reassure me with a comforting hug, after I emerged fully clothed from the behind the curtain.

We went to tell our families and they shared in our excitement. Two babies, wow! My ninety-five pound mother actually picked me up and twirled me around in her driveway, laughing and squealing with delight! After that, the anticipation of the miracle overruled my anxiety.

Mom had a way of turning a negative or scary situation into a positive and exciting one. She saw the adventure in things. Maybe it was all the practice she had throughout her life, making lemonade from lemons.

Three years earlier, Tim and I waited for her to return from her second shift factory job, so that we could break the news of our unexpected first pregnancy. I was a few weeks from graduating high school. And Tim still had another year to go. It wasn't morning sickness that made my stomach turn flip flops while we waited for her arrival, and tried to decide what words could soften the blow we were about to deliver. When I told her, she seemed concerned. She was quiet for a moment, hesitating before reacting to this life-changing news.

But instead of the extreme disappointment I expected, there was a gleam of anticipation in her eyes, as she hugged me and said, "We have a lot of planning to do. There's going to be a baby, and I'm going to be a Grandma. A baby is always a blessing." What beautiful grace she gave us in that moment of uncertainty and shame.

Things were quite different with this pregnancy. Right away, the "stretching pains" were much stronger than with the first, sometimes bringing me to my knees. The sickness was much, much stronger! I was in and out of the hospital for excessive vomiting. I vomited every hour at least, sometimes more. There was no relief. I was showing right away too. And I do mean *right away!* One day I went to get a haircut at the local beauty parlor, where my baby bump was the object of scrutiny among those who feel duty- bound to know the latest news.

"How far along are you?" the beautician wondered.

"Two months," was my shocking reply. "I'm having twins."

"Are you sure there's only two in there?" she said in disbelief.

Then I ran outside the back door, through the gaggle of newsbearers to promptly vomit just outside the salon, with dramatic flair, of course.

We just thought, *This must be how it is to carry twins.* We had nothing to measure our experience against, and assumed my symptoms were typical. My stomach grew at warp speed! By the time I reached mid-pregnancy, I was very uncomfortable, and although I was only about 20 weeks along, my uterus was measuring 43 centimeters. The average size of a uterus for a pregnant woman (carrying a single child) at term (40 weeks) is 40 centimeters. No wonder I was uncomfortable!

Ginny and I were shopping in Wal-Mart with our kids when I was about twenty-two weeks along. I waddled through the aisles, searching through the little boys' underwear department, hoping to find something to inspire our little potty trainer. My back ached, which was hardly anything new. Slowly, the achy cramps spread from my back around the front of my abdomen. No stranger to pre-term labor, I recognized the increasingly noticeable contractions. I had spent many days taking terbutaline to stop labor and control my irritable uterus during my pregnancy with Timothy.

Ginny scooped up our children and rushed our entire troop on the half hour journey to the obstetrician. They hooked me up to the monitors and determined that my uterus was indeed contracting regularly. I was only half way through the pregnancy! While inexperienced in the area of twin pregnancy, I knew that this was way too soon! A foreboding fear consumed me. The doctor told me that we needed to go to the hospital immediately. I looked at Ginny, afraid to leave the doctor's office, afraid at what might come next. I leaned against the wall, shaking and crying.

Time seemed to stop for me in the hallway, or at least I wished I could make it stop. I told Ginny I needed to wait just a minute. I didn't want to take the next step, didn't want to leave the hallway. I just wanted to take a few breaths, without moving. No rounding the corner. No moving toward what lay ahead.

Ginny was always so strong. I don't remember what she said, but somehow she got me to go over to the hospital. It must have been an instinctual fear that something ominous was lurking around the bend. I had no idea what I was about to face. Praise the Lord that in His great mercy, He does not reveal everything to us. Otherwise, nothing Ginny said would have moved me to take the next steps. I would have run the other way, desperate to escape what was to come. But there would be nowhere to run from our destiny. Sometimes the only way out is through. Sometimes what we think we need isn't even close to what God has in store for us.

"For my thoughts are not your thoughts, neither are your ways my
ways," declares the LORD.
"As the heavens are higher than the earth, so are my ways higher
than your ways and my thoughts than your thoughts."
-Isaiah 55:8-9

When we arrived at the hospital, I was hooked up to machines to monitor my contractions, which were becoming more regular. I was given a medication called magnesium sulfate to stop the labor. While this medicine is often effective at stopping or slowing labor, it also causes some unpleasant side effects. It was very irritating to my digestive tract. I was vomiting so much, that my esophagus became torn and ulcerated. Soon, I was only able to vomit bile and blood. The medication slows your body systems down so that you are unable to walk or even move very well. I needed help even to go to the restroom, as the effects of magnesium sulfate left me mostly confined to the hospital bed. I was on the medication for about a week while they continued to battle my labor. Due to the pain and constant vomiting, I did not allow visitors to enter my room. It was a humiliating state; not to mention the concentration it took just to keep from throwing up the contents of my stomach. I only wanted Ginny, my mother, or Tim there.

The nurses at the small hospital were so kind. They would hear me vomiting and come, always with a cold cloth. They would hold back my hair and speak soothing words to me. Sometimes I would even push them away and ask them to go, not to touch me. I was very ashamed to be sick in front of them. They were so compassionate, though. They never left my side.

As I sat in the bed, I prayed constantly, listening to the women in labor in the surrounding rooms. I prayed throughout their cries of pain. Then, shed tears of joy and relief as I heard each baby let out those first precious cries. It sadly occurred to me that if my babies were born right now, they would not be able to cry.

How inconceivable and horrible that revelation felt, to be denied the sounds of your newborn baby's first cries.

I prayed for them and for me, "Please, God, save my babies."

When one of the nurses came to give me a midnight dose of meds, I stopped her to ask the question weighing most heavily on my heart and mind.

"If my babies were born right now, would they be able to cry?"

She shook her head somberly as she dropped her gaze to the floor, and softly replied, "Probably not."

The time came for our scheduled ultrasound. My labor had slowed down and the wretched medication was stopped. I was feeling a little better, and my mood was upbeat. I was joking with the nurses as they pushed my wheelchair along to the ultrasound room. One was teasing me that she liked me better when I was on the mag sulfate and unable to talk! They wheeled me down the hallway into a yellow room. A nurse helped me on to the table, and the technician began performing the ultrasound.

As I lay on cold, flat surface, while she moved the wand over my jelly-covered belly, a feeling of dread came over me. I could sense a change in demeanor from the ultrasound technician.

"Is something wrong?" I asked.

She wouldn't give me a straight answer. In fact, she didn't give me any answer. The color drained from her stoic face, and she wouldn't make eye contact with me. She said that the doctors would explain everything. The technician, the room, the machine, the sheets on my bed, my own skin, everything … except the bright yellow walls … turned gray. A dark, choking fear surrounded me. I could feel a lump of terror rising in my throat. Everything was spinning. The tears streamed down my face, as I struggled against the suffocating fear.

When the nurses came back for me, not realizing that everything had changed, they tried to joke with me some more. They were asking me if I felt better now that I had an ultrasound. I shook my head, unable to find my voice, swallowing the lump rising in my throat thick and heavy.

"Something's wrong." I choked out.

"Did the technician tell you something's wrong?" asked the nurse.

"No, but I could tell by her face, and she wouldn't tell me what it is. But I just know something is wrong." I could barely breathe.

The nurses called my doctor to come and review the ultrasound, to set my mind at ease. The events that followed are a blur to me, and I cannot remember the exact words of the doctors. The memories come in flashes, the words in short bursts. I remember hearing phrases like, "problems with the babies." "One baby has a lot of fluid in the amniotic sac." "Possibly a problem the heart of one of the babies." I can see their faces … the mixture of compassion and helplessness. They said they were sending me to a high-risk specialist first thing in the morning. Tim was there, listening to the foreign words, but he too is a blur to my memory.

That night, I talked with the nurses who had held my hair while I vomited over the course of the week or two I spent in the hospital. They were so caring and concerned. I shared with them that I knew the Lord and that I knew He would see us through. Some said they would put me on their church prayer chain, and several hugged me. I remember a cute red-haired nurse especially, whose heart was touched by our predicament during her time caring for my frail body and the sweet babies growing in my womb. I don't remember her name, but I can still see her freckles and the warmth in her eyes. Eyes that don't look away from the things that are tough to see. Eyes that reveal a heart courageous enough to feel compassion, even when it hurts.

I couldn't sleep most of the night. In between praying, I called some of my girlfriends. I wonder if we take the time to consider just how indispensable women are to one another. That night I called my friend, Nicki. We have been friends since we were twelve years old. I used to go to her family dinners at holiday-time and marvel at the bond the women shared as they gathered around the kitchen table. The women in my family didn't do that. We had our laughs, but there was something special in the gathering of women in the kitchen to bake the holiday sweets. We had many adventures together. And she would remain my friend through life's various seasons.

I also called my friend, Peggy, who had been through a complicated pregnancy. She offered some advice that was comforting. Of course, I spent hours on the phone with my mom, collect. (It was still the pre-cell phone era ... at least in the Gerken household.) Sometimes, no matter how old she is, a girl just needs her mom.

And most of all, I leaned on Ginny, who always knew what to say and what not to say. She could sit by my side under any circumstances, knowing when I needed to laugh, or cry, or pray. What a gift Ginny was to me. She actually walked that journey with me. I believe that God has truly blessed women with such special friendships. We can carry one another's burdens, somehow making the load just a little lighter. These women sure helped to carry my bucket.

Rejoice with those who rejoice;
mourn with those who mourn.
– Romans 12:15

Tim picked me up from the hospital early the next morning. I began the day with vomiting, as usual. This time it was the red Popsicle I had attempted for breakfast. The swelling throughout my body made getting ready a challenge, to say the least. Tim had to help me get my socks and shoes over my swollen feet and the place where my ankles used to be. I was dressed from head to toe in pink, wearing one of the few maternity ensembles that could fit over my immense midsection.

By the time we reached the specialist's office, located twenty minutes from the hospital that had served as my home for the past week, I was in a great deal of pain. I could barely walk; I wouldn't even call it a waddle. My attempt at movement was more like a lurching stagger, as I held one arm around my bulging abdomen, gasping both from discomfort and difficulty breathing, caused by my girth. The receptionist thought it would be best to get me a wheelchair, and I agreed.

I was amused and slightly alarmed with Tim's interesting "wheelchair pushing skills"! He was happy to do whatever he could just to see me smile. That's what Tim does. He makes me laugh. Have I mentioned that's why I fell in love with him?

Everything happened very quickly once we arrived at the specialist's office. Dr. C was all business, but he had a resident with him who possessed the gift of compassion and love, with warmth in his eyes, and gentleness in his touch. In minutes we knew that we were having identical twin girls and we had a name for the evil thing that threatened our precious children: twin-to-twin transfusion syndrome. That moment held both joy and sorrow, as we went from expecting twin "babies" to expecting twin "daughters." Immediately, whether in danger or not, we had dreams for them. We now had a vision of who they would be.

Tim smiled and said, "Two daughters! WOW, I'll have to start lifting weights!"

"Why?" I asked.

"To protect them. I'll have to keep the boys away!" he said, grinning.

Once again, he made me laugh in an impossible circumstance. His words also reflected what kind of father he would be to his little girls. He would protect them and treasure them. He would value and love his daughters, guarding their innocence and modesty.

From that moment, I determined in my heart that our babies would be O.K. Sure, the journey ahead might hold some struggles, but we could overcome whatever was waiting for us. We would pray and stay positive, and our girls would be just fine. After all, they were girls, our girls. And, as my mother always said, "Our family boasts a long line of strong women." Our girls would be strong like the generations before them, and they would beat this.

I was admitted to the hospital immediately and hooked up to monitors as they prepared for an amniocentesis procedure that would drain liters of amniotic fluid from my uterus, relieving the twins and my overworked organs from its effects. Soon strange faces surrounded my twenty-one year old body. Probably close to ten residents stood in a half circle around my bed.

Apparently the type of amniocentesis procedure that would be performed on me was, to the students, a necessary learning experience. To me, it was something unknown and threatening. I laid there shaking with uncontrollable chills. Fear overwhelmed me. My teeth were actually chattering, and not because I was cold! The compassionate resident, Dr. Ch., stepped forward and patted my leg. I don't remember the words of comfort he spoke, but I will never forget the kindness of his eyes. He didn't just see a specimen; he saw a frightened mother, and an overwhelmed father. And he acted.

When a pregnancy is diagnosed with twin-to-twin transfusion syndrome one baby receives "too much" fluid, blood flow, nourishment, and the other baby does not receive enough. In simple terms, it's as if the wires are crossed. One form of treatment is to remove some of the amniotic fluid, relieving the stress on the baby and the Mom.

They inserted the needle into my uterus carefully, and because of its enlarged size and sensitive state, I started having contractions that were strong and quite uncomfortable. I wasn't prepared for the strength of the contractions, and fear quickly gave way to pain as I writhed and moaned quietly every few moments. Tim stood beside me, doing his best to offer soothing encouragement. I could see the fear in his eyes. After a large amount of fluid was taken from the sac, the needle was removed. My uterus remained sensitive, so I was monitored carefully.

The doctors gave us literature that explained the syndrome. One of the statistics stated that babies with advanced twin-to-twin have a twenty percent chance of survival. I decided that my babies would be among the twenty percent who made it, and I didn't want to hear much more about it.

I began vomiting again, profusely. This time, however, the nursing staff at the large, inner-city hospital was less attentive and they were not even aware that I was ill. There was a lot of blood in the vomit and it was very painful. My mother alerted the nurses (quite angrily) that I had been throwing up what resembled coffee grounds on an hourly basis (which, in reality was a mixture of pieces of my torn up digestive tract and old blood), and that I needed some care. They started giving me suppositories for the nausea and medication in my IV's, but nothing seemed to be able to stop the relentless retching.

Once mom pointed out my condition to the oblivious nursing staff, a team of doctors and other specialists were sent in to determine the cause of my excessive vomiting. At one point, they even sent a doctor in to ask me why I was vomiting. They wanted to analyze my psychological condition. *Was I causing myself to vomit? Was I having a conflict at home? How was my relationship with my husband?*

My response to the insulting questions as to the mysterious reason for my vomit: "I don't know, doctor. I was hoping you could tell me why I'm vomiting. Isn't that your job?"

Soon a gastrointestinal doctor visited my room and scheduled a test. The test involved having a scope put down my very tender throat, while I was quite awake and coherent. They could not give me a large enough amount of sedative because of the pregnancy. It did not go well, and by that I mean it took five people to hold me down due to the choking sensation one feels when a scope is forced down one's throat. The procedure left me in worse shape than I was before. The pain was great (like having several knives jammed down my throat and into my chest) as the vomiting grew more violent and my already shredded throat suffered more tearing. The test indicated that my esophagus was ulcerated and I had a hyetal hernia, which was aggravated due to the size and weight of my enlarged uterus putting pressure on my upper body. Additional medication was prescribed to help alleviate some of the symptoms.

While I had been receiving fluid from an IV to prevent dehydration for the duration of my hospital stay, the doctors at one point chose to give me nutrients through the IV, because I hadn't eaten for many days. There was also concern about the condition of my liver due to irregularities in the enzymes. Not only were our baby girls struggling for their lives, there was a growing concern for my health as well.

There were times when my breathing was quite labored and my heart rhythm would grow irregular. The palpitations made my heart feel as if at any moment it could leap right out of my chest. It was an uncomfortable and frightening sensation. My 5'3" frame was not holding up well under the weight of the fluid pressing on my organs.

Tim had bronchitis and was unable to visit much for a few days, which was O.K. with me, because being sick and praying for our lives (especially the babies) took more strength than I had. Of course, this gave the medical staff more to talk about … "where *is* her husband?" By then, I had deteriorated to such a point that I didn't even want *him* to see me: only my mother and Ginny. In the moment-by-moment battle against the constant nausea, pain, discomfort, and indigestion I didn't care if anyone came. Visitors were the furthest thing from my mind.

Mom was always getting after those nurses. She took a leave of absence from her factory job to take care of me, and with the help of my mother-in-law, to take care of Timothy. This ordeal had kept me away from Timothy for more than two weeks. He came to the hospital to visit one day, but I could barely lift my head. I missed him, and it was good to see him, but it took so much effort to keep from vomiting for those few moments he was there. A curious two-year-old who missed his mama, he climbed on my bed, pulling at wires and asking, "What's that?" I just didn't have the energy and asked mom to take him home. I knew it would be easier for him than seeing me that way.

The doctors performed a couple more amniocentesis procedures to remove the excess fluid around the babies, and several ultrasounds to monitor progress. I looked forward to the daily ultrasound when I could watch our baby girls on the screen, and I learned about their individual personalities. We named our girls Faith Elizabeth and Grace Katherine. We chose Faith and Grace from one of my favorite bible verses:

For it is by grace you have been saved, through faith —
and this is not from yourselves, it is the gift of God-not
by works, so that no one can boast.
– Ephesians 5:28:

The "bigger" twin was Faith, and the "smaller" twin, Grace. Faith was very still. She quietly sucked her thumb, while Grace swam madly about, always feisty, like her Mom and her Grandmother. Watching her, I developed an image of this spitfire who would fight hard to live. She was small but mighty. Faith reminded me of her Dad, a quiet strength. This I learned while both were nestled in my womb, yet to meet the world. But I knew them because they were my own. We dreamed of pink lace and ribbons and a nursery filled with two of everything.

Much of the rest of my time was spent just trying not to throw up and to endure the discomfort. Tim really missed having me at home. He was afraid for us. After all, there weren't too many twenty-one-year olds facing what we had on our plates. He had to go to work everyday and put on a brave face. One night, he called to say he had been reading in my "twin" book about twin-to-twin transfusion syndrome. He talked about his concern that only twenty percent of babies affected with this deadly syndrome survive. The doubts were creeping in, as his wife's health deteriorated and his baby girls fought for their lives. I told him our girls were going to be O.K., and I didn't want to hear any more about it. The alternative was unthinkable to my young mind.

Churches all over were praying for me and the girls, and we plowed on. After weeks of the vomiting and not eating, I began feeling some positive effects from the IV that brought nourishment to my depleted body. The IV was similar to what someone may get when they are in a coma, I think. Not long after that, just as quickly as the vomiting came … it stopped.

Praise the Lord! The first thing that sounded good to me was popcorn, and no ordinary popcorn, but the kind that you can get in a large bag that tastes like movie theater popcorn. They sold the particular kind I had in mind at the local gas station in our small town. My loving husband (relieved to be able to do something … anything … to finally get me to eat) brought me some and it was delicious, heavenly even. And, much to the perplexed gastro-intestinal doctors' dismay, gas station popcorn was the first food I was able to keep down in weeks. It was wonderful. The other thing that hit the spot, was iced tea with sugar, which I drank in abundance. My mother learned where the hospital supplies were so she could make the tea, and I would never have to wait on the nurses.

After a couple days of gaining strength through both the IV nourishment and my sudden miraculous ability to hold down solid food, the doctors said that I could go home. And finally the hospital stay was over. I was given an appointment with the specialist a few days after my release, to monitor the progress and health of the babies.

Coming home was an adjustment. Timothy had grown

fond of life at Grandma's house and wasn't thrilled to come home to a very tired mother and rules that are non-existent at Grandma's house. My heart ached as I peeled our screaming toddler off my mother in the middle of our driveway. There were bills to pay and decisions to make, housework that had been neglected, and I wasn't strong yet. Tim had to go to work. Mom and Ginny helped us with everything, and I was never left alone. They continued to put their lives on hold in love and service for me.

Did I mention that during this entire ordeal, Ginny was also expecting her second child in addition to the toddler she already had at home? That is an example of what love looks like. We were humbled and grateful by her family's willingness to "lay down their lives for a friend".

I continued to pray and hope. God sustained me with His precious Word and through the friendship of those that love Him. Families at our church donated meals that were delicious and appreciated. The community sent us their love and their prayers in cards and with visits and phone calls. This is how the Lord works. This is what He calls us to do, to be His hands and feet, showing His love through acts of kindness.

My next doctor's appointment was on a Tuesday. Ginny drove me. The doctors were not encouraged by the results of the ultrasound. They gave me a shot of steroids to hasten the lung development of the babies, saying they may be delivered soon. Then they sent me to another hospital to see a pediatric cardiologist, Dr. K., whose compassion and honesty left her footprints etched on my heart.

Faith was showing signs of heart failure. This didn't fully register with me. I couldn't conceive that something fatal or final was possible. That was an unacceptable, intangible impossibility. Still, there was a definite hint of impending doom as the doctor delivered the findings from our visit.

As I lay on the table, Dr. K looked at me thoughtfully for a moment and asked about the names of our girls, Faith and Grace.

"How did you choose the names Faith and Grace for your babies?" she wondered.

I smiled, and said, "Because it's going to take a lot of both (faith and grace) to get through this. And, because it's part of my favorite bible verse."

After Dr. K explained the precarious situation of our baby girls, I went into a side room with Ginny, to allow myself to attempt to digest the reality that maybe one of our babies wouldn't make it. It was the first time the thought occurred to me. *No, it couldn't be. It was too horrible. I couldn't lose one of my children.* I cried with Ginny for awhile, as we sat in the room and we made a few phone calls to concerned family. I told her that I needed a minute before going on.

It is interesting to observe yourself from the outside, in the telling of a story, easier to see the patterns and coping mechanisms we build for ourselves. I needed a few minutes in that room, before I could face a world where the idea of something happening to one of my babies was a possibility. Like hitting the pause button, I waited until the strength gathered to step out of the room, before pressing play, and resuming life.

Both doctor visits determined that I would be delivering the babies soon. I'm not sure how long, but it was only a matter of days before something didn't feel quite right. I do know that I was about 26 ½ weeks into the pregnancy at this point.

I called the doctor to tell him how I was feeling, and he said if I had contractions that were regular to come right away. It was always difficult to feel movement from the babies because of the amount of amniotic fluid surrounding them. But the movements had changed slightly. I fell asleep, rubbing my belly and praying. Peace surrounded me, and I rested.

The next morning I didn't feel any movement from the babies, which happened often, but for some reason, I was concerned this time. Tim had already left for work for the day.

My Mother drove me to the hospital.

Chapter Three
Changed in a Moment

We were not rushing as we drove. Not feeling a sense of urgency. We stopped to get gas. On the drive, I felt the sense of a slight flutter. Was it movement? It was hard to tell. Movements were difficult to discern with all the excess fluid surrounding Faith and Grace. I rested my hand on my abdomen, wondering what was happening with my girls.

When we arrived, they admitted me to the triage area and checked for their heartbeats with the Doppler. I was hooked up to the usual monitors. The nurse assigned to me couldn't find a heartbeat. I smiled and reassured her that is was often hard to find a heartbeat with the Doppler because there was so much amniotic fluid.

"They're in there", I said confidently.

To be safe, the resident brought the ultrasound machine. I can't clearly recall the words she spoke. It may have been "I'm sorry. There isn't any heartbeat." It could have been just "I'm sorry." It doesn't matter what the words were. The meaning was clear. The voice that emerged from my mouth came from the depths of my soul, but it was someone else's voice; a twisted anguished cry that I didn't recognize.

"NOOOOOOOOOOOOO … Please … NO! My babies. My babies are gone!"

This couldn't be. Both of them were gone before I met them. There would be no bedroom with a canopy crib and pink lace everywhere. No daughters for Tim to dote over and protect. No sisters for Timothy. No little girl giggles and Easter bonnets. No long wavy brown hair blowing in the wind, adorned with ribbons streaming behind, as they ran and played in the back yard. No shiny brown eyes lit up at the sight of a new doll on Christmas morning. This couldn't be. But it was. They were gone. They had been ripped unexpectedly from us. I know, I should have expected it, but I didn't. This wasn't going to happen to my children. I had fought and waited and prayed.

Only a few days ago, it was inconceivable to me that we could lose one of our children, and now they were both gone. This wasn't supposed to happen. These were our girls, my girls, girls from a long line of strong women. I felt as if the world had stopped. For me time stood still. My world, in an instant, was a horrible nightmare that I had not even allowed myself to dream, but had come true anyway.

As if it isn't enough to process the unthinkable, somewhere in the midst of my cries, the nurse or resident or some well-meaning soul that is just a faint blur to me now, was trying to tell me that I should go home and wait for labor to begin on its own.

Through the fog, I heard my Mother beside me, and I turned as if in slow motion to hear her say to the nurse,

"Would you want to go home carrying dead babies and wait until labor starts maybe days or weeks from now? No, you're not going to do that to her. She's delivering those babies. She's not going home."

When I was a little girl, my step-grandfather had a small, clear container of liquid mercury. Sometimes, he would get it down and let us swirl it around and watch it separate and turn into little twirling balls of metal. It was fascinating to me as a child … liquid metal … it didn't make sense. That's how the world around me seemed in those moments. Everything and everyone looked like liquid metal, warping, melting, rolling in senseless patterns without definite forms.

I strained to half-listen to the nurse's answer. Through the sea of liquid mercury, I strived to piece together a coherent thought, wondering what our fate would be. Labor. The word cut through the fog again. And slowly understanding permeated. I don't know what I thought might happen, but labor was not on the list. It had never entered my twenty-one year old mind that I would have to endure labor and deliver babies that would never cry, nurse, or fill our house with life. I guess I thought they would just put me to sleep and perform a C-section. *But labor? How would I do that?*

I must have spoken that thought out loud, because someone answered. She informed me that a C-section would be dangerous to me and the babies because of my enlarged uterus. They said they would have to induce labor. I didn't know how something like this worked, and it would never occur to me that a Mother whose babies had died would have to endure labor, knowing that the end result would not be the reward of her baby's precious cries- the sound of brand new life, followed by the sweet baby smell as she nursed at her mother's breast – but only the silence of death. How does one mentally prepare to endure the agony of labor under such circumstances?

I prayed a little, but I was very weak and almost unable. Others were lifting me up in prayer, however, and I soon felt strength and a peace settled over me. I was somehow able to "do the next thing". Later, a friend who had never visited the hospital shared a dream or vision he had of me during this great time of need. Although he had never been to the hospital, he described in perfect detail the delivery room ... the recliner by the window, the snow, the cross above my bed, the white walls, the emptiness I felt. He felt the Holy Spirit leading him to pray for me specifically with a heavy burden. It was almost as if God spoke to his heart the needs of mine.

I was taken to a private room that would have been lovely under different circumstances. I showered and prepared to be induced. I went through the motions numbly, as if I were literally being carried. I stood in the shower, feeling the warm water hit my skin, keenly aware of the sensation and yet, barely feeling anything beyond the cascading water. A pounding on the door and the sound of my mother's voice broke through the haze.

"Are you o.k.?" she asked with a trembly voice that seemed to belong to someone other than my unbreakable mother.

"I'm fine", I replied without considering my answer.

"Good", she sighed, relief replacing the tremble. "It's just that when I need to cry, to really let it out, I do it in the shower." The image of my mother, usually a pillar of strength out of necessity, crying in private, formed in my mind. I can't recall ever seeing my mother cry.

I nodded, dressing numbly in the crisp hospital gown, as if someone were moving my arms and legs for me.

We had to call Tim and tell him. He sped to the hospital, although there was no longer a reason to hurry.

Years later, while attending training to become a birth and bereavement doula, I was struck in remembering the moment I made that phone call. The moment I heard the words, "I'm sorry, there is no heartbeat," I was changed forever. He was changed by my words. My Tim, my love, with his twenty-one-year old, full of hope self. It was that phone call, and my words saying our Faith and Grace were gone, that changed his life forever. I felt desperate in the realization, as I reflected in the class what I had missed in the moment so many years ago. I wanted to go back in time and stop him from answering the phone. I wanted to make it not so, to protect him from what lay ahead. There was no protection from the truth, for either of us.

We called some family members and church members to deliver our sad news. With each phone call, I became more numb, which was a blessing; otherwise I may not have been able to utter the words over and over again. Through that process, I allowed myself to begin to believe that this had really happened.

Once showered, and after the obligatory phone calls were made, I climbed into the bed and was hooked up to monitors. They began the process of inducing labor with medication in my IV. It was a long, painful process, but the nurses were gentle and caring. They did everything they could to make me as physically comfortable as possible. I had an epidural and pain medication, since there was no reason to be concerned for the health of the babies. Some of the medication they gave me was to blur, numb, or help me forget the experience, but it didn't work. I remember every detail and looking back, I'm grateful. You see, my time as the mother of these precious girls was fading and there were so few things that I could do to mother them. I'm grateful I could do something, even if it was just labor.

At some point, I looked out the window and saw the biggest and most beautiful snowflakes I had ever seen. It was the beginning of November, and a little early for the first snowfall of the year. I was filled with peace, as I watched each intricate snowflake sent from heaven above, and I thought of how those perfect snowflakes were like my Faith and Grace, beautiful and unique, created by God. It blessed me. The snow fell silently, peacefully, in stark contrast to the turmoil in my heart. Somehow, I felt like the Lord sent that snowfall as a gift to them and to me. While the snow fell serenely outside, my world was shattered inside. It wouldn't be long now. The peace washed over me, and I turned to face the next thing. The labor. It was long, lasting through the night and the better part of the next day.

Faith was born first. Then Grace. The silence was deafening. There was no cry. Nothing could have prepared me for that silence. They were bruised and broken, but all I could see was their indescribable beauty. I saw them as they were meant to be. They both had long, slender, piano-player fingers on the ends of their dainty hands. Their lips were in the shape of Tim's mouth, and they had dark eyes, that would surely have turned to the deep brown color of their father's and brother's eyes. Faith was much larger than Grace. She had taken the brunt of the syndrome. They were so tiny. Only a little over a foot long, one fit in each of my arms easily. And I held them with Tim beside me, and my mother nearby. We wept together as I choked out a prayer and sang "Amazing Grace."

A kind chaplain entered the room at some point, asking if we needed anything. The doctors tried to explain to me that we would need to plan a funeral and discuss what to do with the bodies – the bodies of my children. This concept was so foreign to me, at the time that I couldn't even digest the thought of having to plan a funeral for my children, my babies. Tim and

I were twenty-one years old, and someone was speaking to us about planning a funeral for our babies in the delivery room – the place of new life.

Funeral. Stillborn. These were foreign words that did not belong in the delivery room where my babies were supposed to be born. *Stillborn.* What an ugly word to attach to your child. It is such an in between, surreal state to be gone before anyone else knew you were here. But we knew. We felt the emptiness that told us they had been here. They had lived.

There was a struggle to deliver the over-sized placenta, which is another symptom of twin-to-twin transfusion syndrome. For a time the doctors worked, and eventually the labor was finally over. We were left to begin a new chapter in our lives.

Loss of this magnitude is one of those defining moments. Life becomes measured in what happened before and what happened after. I immediately felt changed, as if this event had separated Tim and I somehow from the rest of the world. I felt that we had been united in a special way because this loss, although shared by some who loved us, was uniquely ours. Only we could fully understand. The transformation was so great. In time, I felt such a disconnection with the rest of the world that I didn't even recognize myself.

Physically, I felt better than I had in six-and-a-half months. Because of the size of my uterus, the pressure on my digestive tract had made eating unpleasant and sometimes impossible. Now, the pressure was relieved, and as strange as it sounds, I took some pleasure in eating. I had the best chef salad on God's green Earth that night. It's funny, isn't it, how we learn to be the most grateful for things when we've been denied them for a time? It's also strange in the face of such loss that anything can seem like a gift. But that chef salad was a gift and I enjoyed it.

Nurses and other staff members at the hospital prepared a care package for us that included Polaroids of Faith and Grace and tiny diapers and nightgowns. The nightgowns had been hand sewn with love for babies that are too small for regular clothes, many who lost their lives before they took their first breath. They never put the nightgowns on my girls, though. How I wish I could cover them in the picture they gave me, with a blanket or a gown. They look so stark and cold laying there, uncovered. Included in the package were books on grief and the loss of an infant, one of which was *Empty Arms* by Sherokee Ilse.

In the moment, we may not know how important these tiny mementos are. Often the shock and grief are so overpowering that one can't think or see beyond it. The people who take those pictures and take the time to prepare that care package give us something that says our loved one was here. The time we have with them is so short. And, unlike other losses, the loss of an infant is unique in that they are not kept alive with the memories others have to share about their life. There is little time to create memories, and little left behind of these short lives, except, of course the deep hole in our hearts. But having something tangible to remember that they truly did exist, that there is a reason for the pain and the empty feeling left inside, is priceless.

There are not many possessions that I would call precious, but the few tangible items that commemorate their lives are all that I can touch of them, and they are most dear to me. I am grateful to the people that serve others in such a noble way as to care for these dear babies and their families. They make an unimaginable difference. If it were not for their efforts, we would have had nothing that we could hold in the moments that our arms and hearts ached with void; nothing for the moments when the fast-paced world around us seemed to mock us, saying: *Were they ever really even here? What are still you crying about?* Though we have never met some of the people who cared for our Faith and our Grace with such tender dignity, their footprints are forever etched in our hearts.

The time after the delivery is somewhat foggy. My mother stayed with us throughout the labor and delivery, as she had when Timothy was born. She held Faith and Grace.

My father came too, briefly, during my labor. He has swooped in and out of my life from time to time. I call him the "swooper". Never one to rush into overly emotional situations, to this day, I'm not sure if he meant to swoop in during such a tumultuous time. As I'm writing, I find it interesting that he was not there the day I graduated high school, nor the day I walked down the aisle, nor the day I became a mother for the first time. But, he was there on this day. I tried to warn him, when he called to tell me he had swooped in from Chicago, that I would be in labor, so it wouldn't be much of a visit. Several well-meaning people didn't seem to understand that even though Faith and Grace had passed, I still had to go through labor and deliver their frail bodies into this world.

Dad looked up at me after a few moments in the labor room, and while looking out the window, he said, "I feel helpless." I nodded, knowingly, telling him I understood.

And, after an exchange of words I can't remember, he walked out and did something I wish I could have seen. Something that every child of parents who bitterly divorce wishes she could see. Since I was just two years old when they parted ways, it was something I've never seen him do.

He hugged my mother.

And, in that moment, standing in the hospital hallway, speaking words of tender kindness for the first time in decades, they were just two parents, grief-stricken for their little girl.

People were in and out. There are two memories of the remainder of my hospital stay. The first: I remember Tim and I watching a movie and he said something that actually made me laugh. It felt a bit foreign and strange to me, the laugh, in such an unexpected place, when my heart was so heavy with grief. But, it was a welcome escape. What a gift it is to walk through life with someone who can make you laugh in any circumstance. I may not have known what I was doing at the time, but when I chose to marry this man, I made a wise choice.

The second memory is of the moments we spent preparing to leave the hospital. The reality that we would be leaving without hearts full of joy and our arms full of babies struck me and left me with the anguished ache of loss that I would grow to know well. My arms physically ached with the emptiness of not having them with me. I cried that cry that comes from deep within.

How was I going to face the world that kept going when mine had come to a screeching halt? I didn't think it seemed fair that the world should continue about the business of life when the reality of death was darkening my every thought. As they pushed my wheelchair passed the nursery full of the sounds of new life, it was like pouring salt into the open wounds of my heart. I mentioned the ache of my arms to the nurse wheeling me from my room.

She shoved a vase of flowers unto my lap and said tersely, "Here, hold this."

That was my initiation into a life that had been changed forever and a world that would never fully understand.

There were funeral plans to make, but I couldn't think very much about that. It still seemed impossible that we had to plan a funeral for our children. It was just too much to bear or even accept.

There was one thing that mattered to me, though. I wanted Faith and Grace to have pink dresses with lace and ribbons and bonnets on their heads. There had to be pink lace and ribbons at least this once, because we had been denied so many opportunities for all things little girl. Mom called the necessary places, making the plans and announcements that I couldn't. And she shopped for the dresses that I wanted for my sweet daughters. The girls were too small, even for preemie clothes. So mom, ever the resourceful one, looked in the porcelain doll aisle of the Meijer store. It was getting late, and not many stores were open at that time of night. She soon grew discouraged as she searched for just the right dress and couldn't find anything near what I described. Finally, she just stood in the middle of the aisle, hopelessly crying with the desperate tears of a grandma whose twin granddaughters would never fill her house with joy and the tears of a mother whose daughter was broken with grief.

Soon a lady who worked at Meijer walked up to her and asked, "Are you O.K.?"

"No," my mom said, crying harder.

She told the story of our Faith and Grace and their short life, describing the dresses we wanted and the bonnets. And the more she talked, the more she cried. My tiny, larger than life, spitfire of a mother, broken in the middle of the porcelain doll aisle of the Meijer store.

The lady brought a ladder to the aisle and climbed to the top of the shelf where she brought down doll after doll after doll, spreading them all over the floor until my mother saw two of the most beautiful porcelain brown-haired dolls with the most gorgeous pink lace and ribbon adorned dresses and matching bonnets that she had ever seen.

"There — there! That's it! These are the ones!" she said. And that lady whom I've never met hugged my Mom and cried with her in the aisle of the Meijer store. I don't know if she knows it or not, but God used her that night. I believe he sent just the right woman to help my mother. We should never say that God doesn't care about the little things; that He doesn't see our pain; that He doesn't hold every tear we cry. He even cares enough to provide just the right dresses for two little girls that the world never knew. Just in case for a moment we may doubt; we may feel forsaken. We are not.

> *You number my wanderings, put my tears into Your bottle.*
> *Are they not in Your book?*
> *– Psalm 56:8*

> *… God has said,*
> *"Never will I leave you;*
> *never will I forsake you."*
> *So say with confidence,*
> *"The Lord is my helper; I will not be afraid … "*
> *-Hebrews 135b&6*

Tim and I chose a private service to remember Faith and Grace with only our mothers and their husbands present, in addition to Pastor Jim and his wife, Bonnie. I can't remember the service. All I can remember is the emptiness. The sky was cloudy and gray, lifeless, just like I felt. After it was over, I stood at their graveside frozen. *How could I leave them here?* I knew that they were in Heaven with Jesus, but I couldn't make myself leave my babies in this cold, lonely place. Maybe it was too final for me to accept. Maybe walking away meant that I would have to face a world without the daughters that I had dreamed of, and I didn't know how to do that. I just stood there, numb, lost and empty, barely feeling the cold November wind blow through my hair.

Tim put his arm around my shoulders.

I said, "I can't go, Tim. I don't know how to leave them here in this cold place. I can't."

He said, "They aren't here; they're in heaven. And you're not leaving them; they're always with us, in our hearts."

Those words somehow strengthened me enough to say a prayer and, leaning on him to take those steps. Together, we walked away from the tiny, cold grave.

Chapter Four
Tossed About in the Sea of Grief

There is a time for everything, and a season for every activity under heaven: A time to be born and a time to die ... A time to weep and a time to laugh ... A time to mourn and a time to dance ...
– Ecclesiastes 3:1-8

A Time To Weep ...

Grief has many stages. It is different for everyone, and seems to come at will with a life of its own. Sometimes there is no rhyme or reason to the emotions that spill forth. You cannot predict when it will wash over you, although there are certain triggers that you may come to know as you swim in this sea. It is a struggle to visit these places of early grief and to feel the weight of that great sorrow. But for those walking in that place of new grief, it is so important to know that there is a God big enough to carry us through this, that no matter how forsaken we may feel, we are not, that we are not alone, and that we will not remain tossed about in this relentless sea forever.

After saying goodbye to Faith and grace, I faced a sea of grief that seemed to be choking the life out of me. I flailed about those first days. From the moment they wheeled me out of the hospital, past the nursery, and into the world without my baby girls, I felt like I was drowning. I remember one of the first stark realizations that life would never really be the same, that Tim and I would never be the same. At twenty-one years old, we didn't have a lot of experience with death. We had lost grandparents, and that was difficult. But, grandparents are supposed to die. Babies aren't. While most of our peers still partied through careless days at college, we stood over the grave of our babies.

Words cannot describe the ache … the physical ache that began with my arms and went straight to the depths of my heart and soul. If you are walking a similar path, I don't have to describe it. You know it well. I cried buckets of tears. Cried by day and cried in my sleep at night. I would wake up already crying, still reliving the moment I said good-bye to my girls.

My grief was a relentless roller coaster that I could not control or escape. The pain came in great waves, and guilt was waiting for the few moments my mind could wander from the pain. Mom and Ginny took turns staying with me when Tim returned to work. I was never left alone in the beginning. I was too weak and broken to function. The ache for my children was so strong that it overshadowed everything. I wouldn't leave the house, even to get groceries. In fact, I didn't leave the house for a couple months. I didn't answer the phone or the door in the early weeks.

Ginny, my mother, and Tim formed a protective layer between me and the outside world. Flowers came and I would sob. Christmas ornaments in memory of Faith and Grace (born November 3, 1996) were sent from kind-hearted friends. Ginny answered the door. I curled up in sorrow. It seemed so surreal that we were receiving sympathy cards instead of celebratory "Congratulations on the New Twin Baby Girls" cards. My breasts were full of milk, but there were no babies to nurse.

I struggled with going to church. I went, but it was so hard. We had been praying for a miracle, believing for a miracle. And the miracle that happened was not the one we had asked for. I wasn't angry with God. It just felt so tender. The worship songs … the scripture … the prayers. Everything pierced my broken heart, welling up the emotions that were always waiting just below the surface.

Every word the pastor said seemed to mean something else. It just hurt too much to sit there. Maybe I felt rejected. I began to think that if I had enough faith this wouldn't have happened – maybe it was my sin or some lesson I needed to learn. I felt guilty that I couldn't get past my grief because *a Christian should be joyful and hopeful,* I thought. People would give me cards with bible verses meant for comfort, but they were like stabs of pain in my heart instead, reminding me that something must not be quite right with me.

It was so painful to enter the world without the identical twin daughters that should have filled our household with the abundance of all things baby girl. That's what we had been preparing for, hoping for, praying for. Not this emptiness … this silence. Not this agony of missing.

It may sound as if I were grieving without hope. But, you know the truth is, I was just grieving. I knew God was the place to go with my sorrow, and I went to Him. But, the hurt was still there. It didn't leave right away. There was not a quick fix. It needed to hurt. The tears needed to fall. I needed to talk about my babies, to feel the weight of their absence. And, yes … even to wallow a little. As Christians, sometimes I think we expect people to just always feel joyful, as if they are a failure when they feel sorrow. As if they are lacking faith. I really struggled with that.

The thing is our world had been turned upside down. We didn't know which end was up anymore. I often felt guilty that I was so overcome with sorrow, thinking I was a failure as a Christian. When I did feel a moment of joy, I felt guilty wondering what kind of a mother laughs after losing her baby. I learned that guilt is part of the journey. Knowing that didn't make it go away. But in time, God did ease that guilt.

Tim had to return to life and work so there wasn't much time to dwell on his grief. Timothy was young, but he had sorrow and grief as well. He had wanted to see his sisters. And he had so many questions. Conversations with him were probably some of the most healing times, though. He had the faith of a child, and he so readily accepted that Faith and Grace were alive in Heaven with Jesus.

We could talk about what it would be like and what his sisters would get to do in Heaven. Those conversations were actually very joyful, and they gave me great peace. He didn't have the cynicism to question God's promises like the rest of us. Timothy even liked to look at their pictures, and he was never ashamed to talk about his feelings or to share that he had sisters in heaven.

It was refreshing compared to the world around me who wanted to pretend that they were never really here and move on. Looking back, he was only close to three years old when he was going through this time, but he could grasp concepts that many adults cannot grasp. He had (and still has) a gift of deep understanding.

A couple months into the grieving some people thought that I should "be better by now." Life moves on for everyone. And even those that loved me most reached a point where they just wanted me to get better and get on with life. But I wasn't ready, and I just couldn't.

It was an agony with little comfort for a time. I was weak physically, spiritually, emotionally, and mentally. I wanted to do anything to fill the void and ease the emptiness. As soon as the doctor said it was safe, we began trying to have another baby.

I was at church one Sunday morning a few of months after I had the babies, when I started having cramping in my uterus. Tim drove me to the emergency room where they inserted a catheter to fill my uterus with enough fluid to perform an ultrasound. I'm not sure if the catheter was inserted incorrectly, but, it was — for whatever reason — incredibly painful and I cried throughout most of it.

Then they wheeled me to the ultrasound room, and I saw the same yellow walls of the place, where months before, we heard the first dose of bad news about our twins. The place where all but the yellow walls turned gray. You know the saying, "The first cut is the deepest." Well, that must be true, because the moment when you first hear the news that something is wrong is often the most vivid and traumatic memory. That was the moment when our lives changed. That was the first cut. I have heard from others who have lost their children that the first dose of bad news they received stands out for them, too. That bad news is the moment when everything changes.

When I saw those walls, I was overwhelmed and overcome with hysterical sobs and panic. I didn't even want to go in there. That was the same dreaded room where my nightmare began. And I was here again to have an ultrasound. The memories surrounded and suffocated me until I felt like I was choking.

Eventually, she finished the ultrasound, and the results showed that a large mass of placenta had been left inside my uterus following the delivery of Faith and Grace, and was causing a bad infection. They scheduled an emergency D&C procedure to remove the tissue the next morning.

I grew intensely fearful before the procedure, and shook uncontrollably. I was freezing, but no amount of warmed-up blankets could stop my teeth from chattering. Tim was with me while I waited and he kept trying to make me laugh. And, of course, some how, he did. I think he said something about the really tall hospital socks they put on my legs to help keep me warm.

When I awoke from the procedure, I was disoriented. In my mind, I was back in the hospital where our babies were delivered, back in that time and place of silence. It was as if I had just lost them. I was crying that anguished cry from down deep and mumbling "NO", sobbing uncontrollably as if waking from a terrible nightmare. But worse, it was real. When I was coherent enough to notice someone stroking my hair and speaking words of comfort, I saw that it wasn't a nurse, but my doctor, Dr. H. I don't remember what he said, but I remember the concern and compassion in his eyes. He held me like I was a little girl, as I cried in his arms. I will never forget his kindness.

Again, my Mom and Ginny were there to help me and again, the church pulled together and made food for my family.

After the procedure, I still struggled with pain and other symptoms of infection. The doctor determined that I had a condition known as emetritis, resulting from the placenta and other tissue that was left inside me after the delivery of our daughters. This condition, left unchecked, can sometimes be serious or life threatening. It can also cause damage to the reproductive system. In my case, I just felt weak, achy and tired. The infection attacked my body for almost a year. Each visit to the obstetrician brought painful emotions. I was still grieving and longing for a baby to fill my emptiness.

I know my grief was a struggle for my family. At one point I was even feeling guilty for thinking about moving on and feeling better. I actually thought, *What kind of mother moves on with life after something like this happens?* I wondered if living life or feeling joy meant I was leaving behind my little girls, forgetting them. Then I looked over at Timothy pulling on my hand to come play with him and I thought, *What kind of mother doesn't go on with life when this child, the one pulling at her hands to play, needs her and he is very much alive?*

After all, Faith and Grace were better off than all of us. My grief wasn't for them. Angels sing their lullabies and Jesus cradles them in His arms. My grief was for me, and Tim, our parents, and Timothy. God had used Timothy to rescue me and teach me a great lesson once again. What a gift from God he is! I stood up and played with him that day, and each day forward was a baby step to normalcy, with ups and downs along the way.

In the beginning, I felt as if I were drowning. The sea of grief was relentless. Soon I learned to tread water, though and the sea became less rocky as I stopped resisting the waves. One day, I realized that I had learned to swim in this sea. The waves of grief still rushed in at times, but I was learning to be a stronger swimmer.

The old saying "Time heals all wounds" is not a favorite amongst those who have experienced grief. However, there is some truth to the concept of the initial pain easing over time. And, perhaps it's less a healing that occurs as the time passes, but more of a scabbing over. Yes, in time the pain becomes less intense. However, I believe that what's really happening in that time is that *God is working to heal and restore us. You may have heard the analogy that although we cannot see the wind, we can see the evidence that wind exists as it blows the leaves on the trees. We can feel the wind on our face and hear the sound of it blowing past. I think God works in those invisible ways. We cannot see Him, but we see evidence of His work in our lives. We feel the comfort of His presence.*

My friend Dinah gives a great analogy of how God mysteriously works. She likens it to the changing of the seasons. In the autumn the leaves change colors. Often though it is so gradual, so subtle that we don't realize it fully until one day the trees are orange, yellow, red and brown instead of green. In the same way as winter approaches, the leaves fall from the trees. One day, we notice that the leaves are gone. We know they must have been falling for some time, but it was so subtle and gradual that we hardly noticed until one day they were all gone and the land was stark and bare. When spring comes, everything brings forth new life. What once was dead is alive again. And, then one day it happens. You wake up and the leaves have returned once more —green and shiny and new. You can't point to a time when they began to bloom, exactly. You may have seen a bud or two. But it seems that it is sudden. Suddenly, the leaves have returned. This is not so. It was happening all the time, subtle, gradual unseen, changing, restoring life.

That is the best illustration I have heard of the way the Holy Spirit works in us to heal and restore. One day you realize that God has healed you. You are no longer struggling. But you have overcome what once held you captive, be it bitterness, pain, grief, or sin. God had been healing you all along. (from the book *Dreams of You*, 2004, 2008) You couldn't see it, but now you see that

He must have been working while you were struggling. And now, the struggle is over. How did it happen? It is the mystery of His ways.

Some months after saying goodbye to our baby girls, Ginny and I attended a memorial service for people who had lost their babies. We listened as some mothers and even a few fathers stood and shared their experiences of loss, grief, and healing. It was incredible to be surrounded by so many people who had walked this difficult journey. Somehow it was comforting to know that I wasn't alone.

One beautiful couple stood, and told the story of their precious child who had died. The strength and grace of the Lord shone on their faces as the Mother spoke.

She spoke of how she had been reading in Psalm 34 about blessing the Lord at all times. When she held her baby who had died in her arms, she felt the Lord asking, "Will you bless me now?"

She answered, "Yes, Lord, somehow, I will bless you, even now."

Her words blessed me that day. Her faith encouraged me. She let the light of the Lord shine from her to bless us all that day. I would remember and cling to the strength of her faith and the sight of God's grace woven beautifully in the joy in her eyes and the timbre of her soft voice. We've never met, but her words have reminded me that God's grace is sufficient to meet all of our needs. And He is able to lead us to the Rock that is higher than where ever we are: however low in the depths of despair. There is no unreachable place. He is always worthy of our praise, always full of love and mercy, even in the sorrow of the greatest valley. Sometimes I wonder if broken praise may be the most sacred and true of the humble offerings we lift up to Him. I will be blessed by her faith until the day I die.

Chapter Five
Will You Bless Me Now?

I was desperate for another baby to fill my arms, desperate to fill the emptiness left behind by our daughters. I knew they couldn't be replaced, but somehow I thought we could be restored or our loss would be redeemed in some way if our arms and hearts were filled with new life. The ache of wanting a child is an agony for a woman, a mother-in-longing. God recognizes this ache by mentioning women who have experienced loss, or the longing for a child in His word, as in the story of Hannah in 1 Samuel. Throughout the bible God acknowledges the pain of being barren, as well as the pain in losing a child.

It was approximately one year after the loss of our daughters that I conceived again. We were filled with apprehension and hope. Countless prayers covered the little one inside me, as I cried out to our heavenly Father, asking that He would lovingly knit our baby together in perfect health within my womb.

We wanted to feel the joy of expecting another child. And we did feel joy, but it was tainted somewhat. The innocence we once had was stolen from us. Even Timothy, who had longed for a sibling asked me often if this baby would stay. And, no matter how much I wanted to, I couldn't say for certain that this baby would stay. I would tell him that it was up to God. We must always trust that God knows best what to do to take care of us. I had learned that nothing is certain in this frail life. It made me sad that our family had this dark cloud over us, but we tried to rejoice anyway.

The doctors had assured us that the loss of our twins was due to a condition that exclusively affects twins (TTTS), so there was no reason for concern about this pregnancy. And that did calm us, somewhat.

I was sick, as usual, in the first trimester. My stomach seemed like it wasn't growing as large as I thought it should be as the pregnancy progressed, but then I remembered that when I was pregnant with Faith and Grace, my uterus was abnormally large. No normal pregnancy should be compared to that!

At my first doctor's appointment, I was given a pregnancy book and journal. I wrote notes in the margins.

My third and fourth week: Thanksgiving

"I am four and a half weeks pregnant. We didn't even know that you were here yet, but Timothy, your big brother was already praying for you (Mommy, too). His answer came. Now we're just praying for your health and Mommy's and that you stick around for awhile!"

> *I prayed for this child, and the LORD has granted me what I asked of Him.*
> *-1 Samuel 1:27*

Pregnancy after loss is a unique experience. There are many emotions attached and some people have protective measures against those emotions ... coping mechanisms. It is not uncommon to face the pregnancy as if walking on eggshells afraid something may take it away from them. Nothing is certain for someone who has experienced a loss such as this. For most people, a pregnancy means a baby, a child, a joyful experience, and we are free to dream of a lifetime of memories and possibilities. For us, what once meant joy and expectation had come to mean sorrow, loss, pain, and devastation. For us, this pregnancy alone was a miracle and every minute to be treasured because we thought at any moment this frail miracle could disappear.

December 18, 1997
Second Month

"Had my two-week talk at the OB today. We'll get to see you in about 3 ½ weeks. I really hope everything's O.K. Have to take phenergan every four hours to keep food down. Still pretty sick and exhausted."

Third Month

"I'm still pretty nauseous, but it's not as bad as last time, so I won't complain. Can't wait to see the sonogram. Hope everything's going O.K. in there. I'm so thankful for the chance to know you, even if for a short time, hopefully for a long time though. I'm praying for us everyday, baby."

Fourth Month

"Measuring O.K. Still pretty sick. Feeling flutters!"

The day of the long awaited ultrasound had come. I would finally get to breathe a sigh of relief. I had waited for this mid-pregnancy ultrasound to determine it was safe to stop holding our breath. It was my benchmark. If all went well, I may allow myself to think for the first time that there might just be a chance that a baby could be coming.

I was so excited that morning. I called Ginny, as I did most mornings. I was going to see my baby! I had learned when I was expecting the twins how important it was to drink in every moment of a pregnancy, of my child's life. I knew that it was possible that this moment, this day, this pregnancy could be all I would ever know on this earth of this little one.

During the ultrasound, I was told the basics. I knew my doctor would give me a full report later. They had informed me in advance, however, that no news was good news. If there had been a problem, I would have been told immediately. The ultrasound went smoothly and I left with a good report. Everything was going to be O.K. I breathed for the first time in five months!

I gave the good news to Tim and our other loved ones. We breathed a collective sigh, and looked expectantly to the next hurdle.

The next day, we received a phone call.

Fifth Month
"Measuring small. Ultrasound indicates 'problems'."

Bonnie, our midwife, was extremely apologetic.

"I'm not sure how to tell you this," she began hesitantly.

She was sorry that it had taken so long, but there was a problem with the ultrasound and a concern with the baby. This time, ironically, there was not enough amniotic fluid. They did not know why yet, but they would transfer me to a high-risk specialist as soon as possible. This wouldn't be until after the weekend. I would have to wait three days.

My first words were, "NOOOO! You said everything was O.K. How can this be? How do you expect me to tell my husband and my son that this could happen to us again? How can I give this to them again? NOOO!"

Her reply, "I'm so sorry."

Again the hideous unrecognizable cry emerged from somewhere deep inside of me.

Our appointment with the maternal-fetal medicine specialist was in three days – April 7, 1998. His name was Dr. Michael Marcotte. He performed the ultrasound and began explaining some of the possibilities of the inadequate fluid. I remember him saying that it was possible that the baby had not formed kidneys. I can't remember the specific details of what he said, except that the prognosis was not good. The baby could not survive without kidneys. Even worse, the lack of amniotic fluid made it impossible for the baby's lungs to develop properly. His lungs would not be able to function. There is nothing that can be done for the type of defect he suspected, known as Potter's Syndrome.

For the first time, we heard the words, "incompatible with life" in reference to our son.

I once again experienced that choking, liquid mercury feeling as I lay on the examination table. Dr. Marcotte's eyes were calm and concerned. He delivered every word with careful consideration and compassion. As I felt the pain grip my heart, numbness emerged to form a wall of protection. I knew the depth of that pain and I never wanted to be at its mercy again.

I looked over at Tim, and it was as if the light and life had gone out of him. Something died inside him that day. We don't talk about that moment, but I think that protective numbness surrounded him as well, and to an even deeper degree.

We discussed scheduling an amniocentesis as soon as possible to rule out chromosomal defects and the doctor explained the possibility of inducing labor early, terminating the pregnancy. He said that there was basically no chance of survival. It was also possible that remaining pregnant without amniotic fluid could cause distress and physical deformities to the baby.

He told us we could call anytime with questions. I appreciated the gentleness that he showed in those moments and in the moments we had yet to face.

We walked out into the hallway. I stopped, frozen and unable to move forward, unable to take one step into the life that held the hopelessness of the words we had just heard. I stood by the window, looking out into the pouring rain. I watched the raindrops trickle down the window in unison with the tears trickling down my cheeks. *One word sums up what I felt in that moment. One lonely, dark word.*

Forsaken.

In that dark moment, I felt forsaken. Mocked, destroyed, and without hope. For a moment. I didn't want to take another step. Maybe if I stayed right here in this spot, I wouldn't have to face the ugly truth of what was to come. Maybe I could just make time stand still. Only then that would mean never moving on past this day. Sometimes the only way out is through a situation. I'll say it again — sometimes the only way out is through.

All the way home, I slumped in the truck beside Tim, watching the rain. Darkness enclosed my heart. Over and over a voice inside was mocking me, *Where is your God now?* I didn't have an answer for the voice in that moment. I felt defeated.

I couldn't escape the voice or the pain or the harsh reality. I would have done anything I could to spare us that pain. But I couldn't. We would have to tell our parents and loved ones that this was happening to us again. And I felt like I was a failure. I felt forsaken.

We both did.

I wrote in my journal some of my feelings during this time. It was 2:02 a.m.

"O wretched day! The pain and unjustness of the evil of this day overflow from my heart and my brain until I must do something to rid myself of these words.

The words in Lamentations 3 seem so appropriate for this day. – verse 17 You have moved my soul far from peace; I have forgotten prosperity. And I said, 'My strength and my hope have perished from the Lord.' Remember my affliction and roaming, the wormwood and the gall. My soul still remembers And sinks within me …

Although I am overwhelmed with words and seek relief through them, yet there are NONE that will bring relief. I trust the Lord for all His promises and faithfulness. I pray that I remain a faithful, upstanding servant in the face of this trial.

The night is long and relentless in its mockery of me. This blanket of darkness WILL NOT be lifted. And yet, even as I write these words the Lord reminds me that 'Weeping may endure for a night, but joy comes in the morning.' Am I faithless because my heart dares to ask when? When will morning come to the house of my family and stay? How much night must we endure? The cruelness of this is almost unbearable. It would be unbearable if I didn't know that my

God is able. He will not leave me orphaned, despite any outward circumstances. For the first time I know the unconditional love of a Father that will never desert His child. He will stay and vindicate me and mine. This He's taught me to trust with all my heart like no fleshly being ever has or will or can teach me. And in some unexplainable way, I still feel like standing on a mountain and shouting – 'My Father rules the universe. He will not forsake me. He will not allow me to be left in this pit forever. His compassions fail not. He will redeem me. DO NOT DOUBT.

And I am humbled by the fact that through His mercies we are not consumed. His faithfulness is great.

Lord, if you're asking – Yes, somehow, I will bless you EVEN now. Your grace and mercies have already surpassed what justice would bring me, and I know it. On my face, I thank you, and ask for forgiveness if you find ANY pride or wicked way in me. Please take it out. Your servant wishes to honor you with her life. Please cleanse me and make me a faithful servant that blesses you in the face of adversity. Know that any angry words I speak are from the pain and sorrow I cannot help. Yet, please, Lord, I pray for the strength to endure and remain a faithful servant; in all my ways acknowledging You that you may find favor with Your servant.

Lord, my last prayer for now is please spare my family the agony of what seems to lie ahead. Please shield and protect, strengthen, heal, bind together and save this family that You've made grow so dear and precious to my failing, aching heart. Please find the grace and mercy to Heal and Save this child and this family. And thank you for the child and children you have blessed my life with. Please forgive me and protect me and my family for deeds as yet undone out of pain or desperation. Keep us faithful and diligent to Honor You with our lives. Keep us from sin in our anger and sorrow. Protect Timothy and somehow in a mighty way, I ask humbly, KNOWING WITH ALL MY HEART THAT NOTHING IS TOO DIFFICULT FOR YOU, I pray for a miracle that you would heal this child fully and save this child's life for my family and myself. Please hear Your child's earnest prayer. Nevertheless, not my will but THY will sweet Lord. Please remember the agony of our hearts. You are more than able. Praise You. Thank you for NEVER forsaking us.

I love you Lord,
Amen

> *Though he slay me, yet I will hope in him;*
> *— Job 13:15a*

> *Then he fell to the ground in worship and said:*
> *"Naked I come from my mother's womb,*
> *and naked I will depart.*
> *The LORD gave and the LORD has taken away;*
> *May the name of the LORD be praised."*
> *Blessed be the name of the LORD.*
> *— Job 1:20b*

I didn't have an answer at first. That night, as the relentless mocking continued, I reached in my helplessness for my bible. I opened it and let my tears drip on the words … the words that would be my soothing balm, my weapon against the mocking attacks, the truth that would squelch every lie that threatened my hope. As the storm raged on with all of its fury, I collapsed into His arms, wet from the rain … tired … bedraggled … barely even able to reach up and take His hand. It was O.K … my weakness, my inability to put one foot in front of the other. The Lifter of my head was there. He met me there. He met me there as I read the familiar words that quieted that mocking voice.

For He Himself has said, "I will never leave you nor forsake you.
– Hebrews 13:5

Who shall separate us from the love of Christ?
Shall tribulation, or distress, or persecution, or famine, or
nakedness, or peril, or sword?
As it is written, For your sake we are killed all day long;
We are accounted as sheep for the slaughter.
Yet in all these things we are more than conquerors through Him
who loved us. For I am persuaded that neither death nor life,
nor angels, nor principalities, nor powers, nor things present nor
things to come, nor height nor depth, nor any other created thing,
shall be able to separate us from the love of God which in in
Christ Jesus our Lord.
– Romans 8:35-39

His love … nothing can separate us from it. No trial. No sorrow. No loss. No imperfect faith. No inability to measure up. Nothing. Nothing can separate us from the love of God which is in Christ Jesus our Lord. Nothing. Whether we can feel it or not, His love is so powerful - His relentless love for you and for me. And, if you cannot feel it right now, just hold on. You will again, one day. You will. He won't stop until you know how dearly loved you are.

He will never leave me. Even if I feel deserted, He is there. In the thick fog of the unknown, in the darkness of the greatest sorrow, in the depth of the lowest pit … He will never leave me. He is there. And I do not walk alone.

How do I know? Because I walked there, in one of the darkest, loneliest pits of despair. And, He walked with me.

Chapter Six
The Choice

If disaster comes upon us – sword, judgment, pestilence or famine- we will stand before this temple and in your presence (for your name is in this temple), and cry out to you in our affliction and You will hear and save.
– 2 Chronicles 2:9

… For we have no power against this great multitude that is coming against us; nor do we know what to do, but our eyes are upon You.

… Thus says the LORD to you 'Do not be afraid nor dismayed because of this great multitude, for the battle is not yours, but God's

… You will not need to fight. Position yourselves, stand still, and see the salvation of the Lord, who is with you …

After the initial shock of devastating news, it was time to focus on the next topic presented to a couple in this situation – The Choice – whether or not to terminate the pregnancy. From a medical perspective, this seemed like the obvious choice. The syndrome that our baby had, known as Potter's Syndrome (absence of kidneys, low amniotic fluid, leading to lung failure, and other related birth defects) was fatal. There would be no chance of survival. To add to the intensity of the situation, the more he grew, the more likely he would be harmed physically due to the limited space caused by lack of fluid. There was a danger of deformities of his limbs and face as well as other areas.

It was Holy Week, when we had to choose the fate our unborn child, our son, as if we were qualified to do such a thing. I was afraid for the pain our family would face once again, and afraid for the possible harm caused to our baby if he were to remain in my womb. We had already stood beside one grave that held our children.

Tim and I wanted to do the right thing. This should be easy, right? I am a pro-life Christian woman, a mother and wife who values family above almost anything. But I also knew the pain and sorrow of the loss ahead. I had walked that dark path of grief.

Could we really endure the rest of my pregnancy – four more months – waiting for our child to die, knowing that just the simple act of growing within me could be harming him everyday? Would he be in pain? Could my choice spare him the pain and spare us the long journey of waiting, only to grieve? Maybe we could move on faster; maybe somehow I could make the burden lighter for my family if I could just make the right choice. But what was that? Before I was presented with this difficult question, I thought I knew the answer. But this was different. This was my child, and my family that had already endured so much sorrow at the loss of Faith and Grace.

My friends surrounded me once more in my time of great need. They sat at my kitchen table – Dinah, Betsy, Becki, and

Ginny. We talked about the seemingly impossible situation my family was facing. These sweet sisters didn't judge me or pretend they had all the answers. They listened and loved me. They prayed and offered what support they could. Looking back on that day, it seemed so murky. The answer was always just out of my reach. I agonized, willing to trust God with many things – but unsure if I could trust Him with this.

As we sat together, the telephone rang. It was my regular OB doctor, Dr. H – not the high-risk specialist. He had heard of the choice my husband and I were being asked to make. He did something doctors rarely do. He told me exactly what he thought I should do.

He said, "If this were my wife and baby, I would terminate the pregnancy. If not, you are only prolonging the inevitable." This was the man who had walked with me through the loss of our twin daughters, who had stroked my hair compassionately when I was confused and consumed with grief after my D and C procedure.

I talked with nurses who had walked through this with us. I wrestled with the image of asking my family to walk through this again, knowing the grief that we had already endured. Could I ask Tim to look at me for four more months, knowing that I carried a baby who would die? And, poor Timothy ... would this be what he thought of when he thought of pregnancy: sorrow, loss, the robbing of joy? Could our family walk through this again? Could we handle the waiting?

I didn't know what to do. And, Tim was fairly quiet on the subject. I cried out to the Lord night and day: praying, weeping, and searching the Scriptures for the answer. And He answered me.

Late one night, as I was reading the Easter story, I came

to the part where Pontius Pilate washes his hands of the Jesus situation. He said he didn't want the blood of Jesus on his hands (Matthew 27:19-24). The Lord spoke the answer to my heart, as I read about Pilate washing His hands of the situation. The decision didn't need to be in our hands. We could just leave it to God. So, we chose to wait, to trust Him to carry us and our baby through this journey.

If you are reading this and made a different choice, whether because of medical necessity, feeling this option was the best for your family, or just not having a full understanding of the options (many doctors don't even present the option to continue), please know that we understand how difficult it is to face this impossible decision, this choice that no parent should have to face. We never approached this path as parents who had all the answers. We were not trying to be heroes and were unaware that we were pioneers forging an unknown path. We were simply parents, doing the best we could for our family in an excruciating situation.

I know that we are all parents who loved and wanted our precious babies. However the path to this point, we are now parents who have grieved the loss of our children. And, there is healing in the arms of the Lord for all of our hurts.

We left the situation completely in God's hands, trusting that He would make a path for us to healing and restoration. Maybe He would even choose to save our son. So, I told Tim what I had read and how I thought it was God's answer to our difficult question. He agreed and we "chose" to put the situation in God's capable hands, trusting Him to care for all of us.

As I continued to focus on my Savior's journey to the cross on that Holy Week, I felt that I was taking my own journey.

We are supposed to pick up our cross daily, die to ourselves daily, that we may follow Him and live in Him. But this was the biggest cross I had been asked to carry so far.

The mocking questions sometimes grew so loud, *Where is your God now?*

I wondered; does He understand my pain? I felt guilty for the struggle it was for me to trust and obey. Then on another late night, while searching His word for some answers, He revealed this to me:

I couldn't sleep that night. The tears wouldn't stop. The pain wouldn't subside. There was no where to find relief. Desperate for comfort. Desperate for hope. Just desperate, I searched the scriptures, struggling to read through my tears. "Jesus is my example," I thought. "Show me, Lord. Show me the way to walk this path. I want to please you … I want to trust you … but I don't want to lose another child. My heart is broken … "

The first verses I read were in Hebrews 12:2 … looking unto Jesus, the author and finisher of our faith, who for the joy that was set before Him endured the cross, despising the shame, and has sat down at the right hand of the throne of God. Two truths slammed into my heart. 1. Jesus endured the cross, despising the shame. It wasn't easy for Him. 2. He did it for the joy set before Him. There was a purpose … our salvation and His glory. There would be joy on the other side of the suffering.

Then, I looked to Luke 22:39-44 and focused for the first time on the agony of my Savior. What did He do when He was in agony? He prayed. He asked the Father three times **"Father, if it is your will, take this cup away from Me."**

*Then He said, "**nevertheless not my will, but Yours be done.**" Then, an angel appeared and strengthened Him. **And being in agony, He prayed more earnestly. Then His sweat became like great drops of blood falling on the ground.** (verse 44)*

This was our Savior, our Redeemer, our King ... in agony. What did He do? The more agony He felt, the harder He prayed. He poured out His requests to the Father, but inevitably trusted the Father for what was best. Faith. Trust. Abide. Humble to the Point of Laying Down His Very Life. He accomplished the task, and all the while, He kept His eyes on the prize ... the "joy that was set before Him."

He rested in the promises of the Father. Was I faithless because I didn't enjoy the cross before me- because I despised the shame? No, even my Lord despised the shame. But He obeyed anyway because of His great love. Was it possible that I could look to Him, the author and finisher of my faith as an example? My Lord had looked past the cross, believing that the joy set before Him would be revealed. That was what I needed to do.

"Oh, Holy Spirit enable me.

Not my will, but thy will be done, Oh Lord."

Sixth month

"Amnio shows normal genetic make-up of baby – Thomas. Unsure of reason for low amniotic fluid. Praying for a miracle. Thomas is moving, feeling kicks."

There was such a low amount of amniotic fluid that they had to add fluid to remove fluid from the amniotic sac to perform the amniocentesis. I know that doesn't make sense, but that's what happened. As I lay on the table watching the ultrasound machine, all that I could see on the screen was Thomas' face. He was facing me, as if we were looking directly into each other's eyes. The world around us faded away for a few moments, and it was just Thomas and me- a Mother and her son looking into each other's eyes. I was flooded with love for this little one, this child who was my own. I knew that we had made the right choice in that moment. This was my son and that was all that mattered. I had to trust that God would take care of our son and our family. It was the only choice.

Chapter Seven
Manna in the Wilderness

"… But you are a forgiving God, gracious and compassionate,
slow to anger and abounding in love … "
"Because of your great compassion you did not abandon them
in the desert. By day the pillar of cloud did not cease to guide
them on their path, nor the pillar of fire by night to shine on the
way they were to take. You gave your good Spirit to instruct them.
You did not withhold your manna from their mouths, and you
gave them water for their thirst. For forty years you sustained
them in the desert; they lacked nothing, their clothes did not wear
out nor did their feet become swollen."
– Nehemiah 9:16 & 19-21

The next four months tested our faith constantly. We prayed fervently for a miracle, hoping and wishing, fearing that staying pregnant could be causing physical harm and deformities to our baby. It was a great strain on our family. I spent time planning our son's funeral, and yet, still somehow hoping that God would give us a miracle and save him.

The battle was everyday, moment-by-moment. I struggled each morning, thankful that I had another day with this child, praying, pleading agonizing, wondering. I searched the scriptures. I battled the doubts, the pain, and the excruciating disappointment. There were moments when I wondered if it was some unrecognized sin that had brought this calamity on my family. Was there some lesson that we did not learn the first time? Was it my unbelief and doubt that may prevent healing for my child? Was it my lack of faith that was causing this?

I knew during our "Holy Week" journey when we faced the choice to continue this pregnancy that part of the path we would walk included being in public with a growing pregnant belly in a small community where people know if you so much as sneeze. I knew it would mean having our four-year-old son, who had already lost his two sisters, look at me everyday for the next four months knowing that the baby inside me, his brother, would be born - only to die. I knew that I would be a walking reminder to my husband, our parents, and my friends of what tragedy was to come. But I never could have predicted how difficult that would be.

It is horrible to say, but during darker moments, I felt like I represented a coffin, carrying this child that they said was doomed to die. I felt like a black cloud on my family. How could they even want to look at me? At other times, I treasured every moment, soaking in the gift of life that I was carrying, remembering that he still lived. I sang to him and prayed over him, loving him as we waited for the unknown. I wish I had embraced every moment, never allowing the dread to creep in. But, I walked this path the best I could. I mothered the best I could, under these unique circumstances. Even as I write the raw truth of some of the hardest moments on this journey, please know that I never, for one second, felt regret for our choice to continue our pregnancy, to embrace life with Thomas for however long he was with us.

There's also the situation of going to the grocery store where well-meaning people approach to touch your stomach and congratulate you on what they perceive as a great joy- new life growing inside of your womb. How blessed you are! They do not know that every minute you are wondering if your baby is suffering inside or if he's going to make it through the day.

One day at the swimming pool, Timothy was playing in the water when a child came up to say "Congratulations on your baby, Mrs. Gerken. Is it a boy or a girl?"

I tried to smile as I choked out, "It's a boy."

The little girl asked Timothy, "Are you excited that you are having a brother?"

He looked at her and said flatly, "He's sick and he's probably going to die."

It was one of the most hideous moments of my life. That was what my son knew of the meaning of pregnancy and having siblings. There aren't words to describe what that did to my mama-heart, or how desperately I wished I could protect him from the reality that his tender young heart was exposed to as we walked this path.

I remember the moment we told him that something was wrong with the baby and he probably wouldn't make it. It was a difficult decision to make, but it didn't seem fair to allow him to expect a sibling for four months and then feel shocked when he died.

I pulled him aside gently, and tried to hold back my tears as I explained that Thomas was very sick. He would only be with us for a little while, and then he would probably go to heaven to be with Jesus. Then he wouldn't be sick anymore.

Jesus would make Him well in heaven.

He looked at us and said in a quivering tiny four-year-old voice mixed with sorrow and anger, "So I won't get to hold him, then. I won't get to hold my brother. He won't stay."

"I'm so sorry, honey," I cried with him as I pulled him into my arms.

We talked about God being able to heal and how we could pray everyday and trust that God would do what was best. He may choose to heal the baby or He may choose to heal our broken hearts, or both. We talked about heaven and eternal life with Jesus.

I wondered, W*as it enough to think that God could heal our baby or were we expected to believe with complete confidence that He would heal our baby?* That seemed a little presumptuous to me. But I wondered about this faith thing. *Was my lack of faith the reason for all of this agony? If I could just learn the lesson somehow, would we be spared?*

These questions plagued me night and day, which prompted me to search the scriptures even more. I wanted to believe. I wanted to trust the Lord completely. But how? What exactly does that mean?

It was while wandering in this wilderness that I began to feast on the manna that is straight from heaven – The Word of God.

What is faith?

> *Faith is the substance of things hoped for,*
> *the evidence of things not seen.*
> *– Hebrews 11:1*

In Hebrews chapter 11 many examples of faith are given. I wondered if the people described in scripture ever faced doubts or questions in their journey through faithfulness. Abraham, Enoch, Isaac, Noah, Jacob, Moses were mentioned as faithful followers of God. David was called a man after God's own heart. I looked back at the stories of each of these men and some women. None of them were perfect. They only trusted God. There were moments in each of their journeys when circumstances seemed to contradict the truth. They abided with Him anyway. But some of them even took matters into their own hands for a moment. Some of them fell for a time. Were they forsaken? Were they no longer useful for the Kingdom of God? No. As a matter of fact, somehow these imperfect people are still counted as faithful. They still knew where to turn, even in moments of doubt.

And without faith it is impossible to please God, because anyone who comes to him must believe that He exists and that he rewards those who earnestly seek him.
I wanted to please God so badly. I wanted to be found faithful and worthy. But how? I believed that He existed and I was earnestly seeking Him. Was that enough?
For he (Abraham) was looking forward to the city with foundations, whose architect and builder is God.
— Hebrews 11:10

I read on as the Bible described more examples of faith in verses eleven and twelve.

All these people were still living by faith when they died. They did not receive the things promised; they only saw them and

welcomed them from a distance. And they admitted that they
were aliens and strangers on earth. People who say such things
show that they are looking for a country of their own. If they had
been thinking of the country they had left, they would have had
opportunity to return. Instead, they were longing for a better
country — a heavenly one. Therefore God is not ashamed to be
called their God, for he has prepared a city for them.
– Hebrews 11:13-16

I continued to read about the faith of Abraham and Sarah, Isaac and Jacob, Joseph and Moses in verses 16-25.

He (Moses) regarded disgrace for the sake of Christ
as of greater value than the treasures of Egypt,
because he was looking ahead to his reward.
– Hebrews 11:25

Hmmm, that sounded familiar. I read on to verse 32.

And what more shall I say? I do not have time to tell you about
Gideon, Barak, Samson, Jephthah, David, Samuel and prophets,
who through faith conquered kingdoms, administered justice,
and gained what was promised; who shut the mouths of lions,
quenched the fury of the flames, and escaped the edge of the
sword; whose weakness was turned to strength; and who became
powerful in battle and routed foreign armies. Women received
back their dead, raised to life again …

Verse 38 … the world was not worthy of them.
They wandered in deserts and mountains, and in caves
and holes in the ground.

These were all commended for their faith,
yet none of them received what had been promised.
God had planned something better for us so that only together
with us would they be made perfect.
– Hebrews 11:39 &40

They walked with the Lord. They obeyed what He asked. They trusted Him even though they did not see the promises; they believed anyway. They faced obstacles; they relied on Him. They were imperfect; His grace was sufficient. They had moments of doubt; they endured by trusting Him. They grew weary for a moment; He encouraged them to continue on.

As I read, I began to understand that it is God who works in us through the power of the Holy Spirit. Our job is only to look to Him.

Therefore, since we are surrounded by such a great cloud of
witnesses, let us throw off everything that so easily entangles and
let us run the with perseverance the race marked our for us.
Let us fix our eyes on Jesus, the author and perfecter of our faith,
who for the joy set before him endured the cross, scorning its
shame, and sat down at the right hand of the throne of God.
Consider him who endured such opposition from sinful men,
so that you will not grow weary and lose heart.
– Hebrews 12:1-3

It was as if He was speaking directly to me. Jesus was the One I should look to. He endured the cross, scorning the shame. Why? How? Because of the joy set before Him. As I sat there studying and praying, I was reminded of Romans 8:18

For I consider that the sufferings of this present time
are not worthy to be compared with the glory,
which shall be revealed in us.

Faith begins with where our eyes are looking and who our hearts are trusting. God had a plan and a purpose for us. God was (and is) able to carry us through, but even more, He would reveal glory in us. He would use our pain and suffering to reveal and glorify Himself and He would somehow heal and restore us. **Maybe faith was partly accepting whatever He gives and believing Him whatever happens. It is less about our circumstances and our performance and more about who He is and what He is able to do through us, if only we seek and obey Him.**

Through His word we learned that faith goes hand in hand with obedience. Believing isn't enough; we must abide in Him. **Faith is trusting what we don't see, obeying when we don't understand, earnestly seeking God's truth, and fixing our eyes on Jesus, the author and perfecter of our faith.**

Being confident of this, that He who began a good work in you
will carry it to completion until the day of Christ Jesus.
– Philippians 1:6

How is that work perfected and completed?

Consider it pure joy, my brothers, whenever you face trials of
many kinds, because you know that the testing of your faith
develops perseverance. Perseverance must finish its work so that
you may be mature and complete, not lacking anything.
– James 1:2-4

And the God of all grace, who called you to His eternal glory in Christ, after you have suffered a little while, will Himself restore you and make you strong, firm, and steadfast.
— 1Peter 5:10

God uses the struggles we face. He uses our pain to draw us to Him and to complete the good work he started in us. He grows us and establishes us, teaching us to abide in Him. He never wastes anything in our lives … not the pain, the sorrow, the joy, not even our own weaknesses, failures, victories, and sins.

I wanted to know what Jesus would do. I wanted to look to Him as my example and be taught His ways.

I prayed, "Lord, show Yourself to me. Teach me how to be faithful. Give me the strength."

And He did, day-by-day, verse-by-verse.

I was studying the gospel of John when I reached the story of how Jesus raised Lazarus from the dead. In chapter 11, Jesus responds to the news that Lazarus is ill by saying:

This sickness will not end in death. No, it is for God's glory so that God's Son may be glorified through it.
— John 11:4

Well, being a mom, with an aching heart, hoping with every part of my being for a miracle from my Lord, I was excited by this verse. Was God speaking to me, telling me that he would not let my son die?

I read on to verses 25&26 when Jesus says:

*I am the resurrection and the life. He who believes in me will live, **even though he dies;** and whoever lives and believes in me will never die. Do you believe this?*

*Yes, Lord … I believe this … and I finally understood. Over the course of a few days, the message sunk in — no matter what the outcome, **Thomas will live.*** God whispered to my heart, whether Thomas was healed physically on this earth or whether He was made complete in heaven, He would live. He would live, and his life would be a miracle … no matter what. So … I **was** expecting new life. New beautiful, amazing life. God whispered this promise to my heart in the quiet of my kitchen as my tears dripped onto the bible before me.

It was like a lightening bolt! He was reminding me that circumstances didn't matter. My son would not die no matter if his earthly body ceased to live or not. Did I believe that because of Jesus' death, we would not die, but have eternal life? Could I trust that my son lived on, whether on Earth or in heaven? Could I trust that God's grace would be sufficient for any circumstance? What mattered was where my trust was. Who was the source of my strength? Where were my eyes fixed? Jesus wanted my eyes fixed on Him, not our circumstances. I had to accept this by faith because I didn't fully understand how to do that on my own. The best part is, I didn't have to.

Believing Without Seeing

In this you greatly rejoice, though now for a little while, you may have to suffer grief in all kinds of trials. These have come so that your faith — of greater worth than gold, which perishes even though refined by fire — may be proved genuine and may result in praise, glory and

honor when Jesus Christ is revealed. Though you have not seen him, you love him; and even though you do not see him now, you believe in him and are filled with an inexpressible and glorious joy, for you are receiving the goal of your faith, the salvation of your souls.
– 1 Peter 1:6-9

It seems that God often works in themes when He's teaching us. I was thinking about the latest theme, "believing without seeing" that He had been revealing through His Word, while we waited to meet our precious son. As I continued to study in the book of John, I came to the part just after Jesus had risen from the dead and was appearing to his disciples in chapter 20.

Now Thomas (called Didymus), one of the Twelve, was not with the disciples when Jesus came. So the other disciples told him, "We have seen the Lord!"
But he said to them, "Unless I see the nail marks in his hands and put my finger where the nails were, and put my hand into his side, I will not believe it."
A week later his disciples were in the house again, and Thomas was with them. Though the doors were locked, Jesus came and stood among them and said, "Peace be with you!" Then he said to Thomas, "Put your finger here; see my hands. Reach out your hand and put it into my side. Stop doubting and believe."
Thomas said to him, "My Lord and my God!"
Then Jesus told him, "Because you have seen me, you have believed; blessed are those who have not seen and yet have believed.
– John 20:24-29

I thought of all the people who praise God when things are going well, saying, "God is so good!" That is true and we should praise Him at all times and in all places (Psalm 34:1). **But I was learning that God is still good when things do not go as we want them to go. And He is always worthy of our praise.**

We chose the name Thomas for our son because through this journey, we learned about believing God without seeing. We learned that being faithful doesn't mean not feeling doubt or fear. Faith is believing God's promises, clinging to His truth anyway, when you're most afraid and filled with doubt and questions. Still believing when the answer is not what you want to hear or when there seems to be no answer at all.

Chapter Eight
His Grace is Sufficient

Three times I pleaded with the Lord to take it away from me.
But He said to me, "My grace is sufficient for you,
for my power is made perfect in weakness."
– 2Corinthians 12:8&9a

Seventh Month
*Thomas has 2 cm of fluid and was "practicing breathing" at 28 weeks. Praying daily for a miracle. **All** is in our mighty Father's hands. Thomas is weighing in at 2.1 lbs.*

I continued to struggle to trust and get through each day, carrying the desires of my heart to God. I lived from one doctor's appointment to the next. I clung to the fact that I would at least get to see (via ultrasound) that Thomas was O.K.- for now. I knew that as he grew, he could be harmed by the limited space. Because of the lack of space, I rarely felt his movements. It was reassuring to watch him on the screen, knowing that his heart was still beating. I also knew that this pregnancy may be the only time I spent with this child and I wanted to see him on the ultrasound screen as much as possible.

I searched on the Internet for any unique cures for Thomas's condition. And we even went to the University of Michigan in

Ann Arbor to see if anything could be done to save our baby. I remembered the guilt I had struggled through after we lost Faith and Grace, thinking: *Had we done enough to save them? Was there some doctor with a miracle cure?*

I explained my feelings to Dr. Marcotte who always took time to answer my difficult questions or had the patience to care and reassure when there was no answer. I would even show him some of the ideas from the Internet and he was always gentle, carefully considering every response. He had an exceptional gift that many doctors lack. It must be difficult in their profession to handle a situation like mine, one that seemed to have no answers. Those in the medical profession are used to having an answer. Doctors are in the business of healing, curing, and restoring. In my circumstance, Dr. Marcotte couldn't cure what we had. He had to wait helplessly with us.

He chose to feel compassion and understanding rather than indifference. It is so rare for someone in his position to allow himself to remain vulnerable to the things that are hard and painful and ugly. He allowed me to get through that time my way. He was able to tell me a hopeless thing in a way that still allowed me enough hope to get through it. I don't know how he did that, but he did. He made himself available to me when my doubts and fears were overwhelming or even if there was something I just didn't understand. He is an exceptional person and an exceptional doctor. For choosing to have the courage to show compassion and walking this journey alongside us, his footprints are forever etched in our hearts.

Eighth Month
Here we are. This part of the journey is coming to an end. Thomas weighs 4lbs. according to the ultrasound. Still praying and waiting,

trusting our Father to take care of us all. His ways are higher than ours. And His love for us is inconceivable. We're in good hands.

My birthday was Sunday, July 12th. I was scheduled to be at the hospital on Monday July 13th. Ginny and Dinah, along with Tim and some other friends decided to surprise me with a birthday party at Dinah's house. She gives the best parties. You are always comfortable and welcome at Dinah's house. It's one of her many gifts. She has made an art out of creating a safe haven in her home. She taught her beautiful daughters to do the same, and also passed the gift on to me.

That afternoon, we laughed together and shared joy and peace despite the storm ahead. I am so grateful for these precious friends.

I had wondered from the moment we heard the words "incompatible with life" how we would face another labor that ended without the sounds of a newborn baby cry. I wondered if carrying Thomas was causing him harm. Wondered what we would be faced with the day we met our sweet boy. And, my answers would come soon.

I was admitted to the hospital to induce labor at about 38 weeks gestation. My labor was long and intense. Contractions came fast and hard, but were not effective. I dilated slowly, as I labored throughout the night. The waves of pain were like nothing I had experienced before. The nurses were unsupportive and without compassion, which seemed so strange, given our circumstances. Tim was unable to offer much assistance. What could he really do anyway? If you were looking with your eyes, it would seem I was alone to face the giant before me, but I wasn't really, not at all.

I began to pray, and with each contraction I quoted scripture. It probably seemed crazy to hear me mumbling scripture through attempts to use Lamaze breathing methods. I just talked to God all the way through. All of the struggles that had led up to this moment, all of my searching had prepared me. I was at my weakest, in the time of greatest need. But I knew where to look for strength.

> *I lift up my eyes to the hills — where does my help*
> *come from? My help comes from the LORD, the Maker of*
> *heaven and earth.*
> *He will not let your foot slip- he who watches over*
> *you will not slumber; indeed, he who watches over Israel will*
> *neither slumber nor sleep.*
> *The LORD watches over you- the LORD is your shade*
> *at your right hand; the sun will not harm you by day,*
> *nor the moon by night.*
> *The LORD will keep you from all harm — he will watch over*
> *your life; the LORD will watch over your coming*
> *and going both now and forevermore.*
> *– Psalm 121*

> *Hear my cry, O God; listen to my prayer.*
> *From the ends of the earth I call to you/ I call, as my heart grows*
> *faint; lead me to the rock that is higher than I.*
> *-Psalm 61:1-2*

> *My soul finds rest in God alone;*
> *my salvation comes from him.*
> *He alone is my rock and my salvation;*
> *he is my fortress, I will never be shaken.*
> *-Psalm 62:1-2*

When I could no longer read scripture because of the pain, I began reciting from memory.

I became very ill at one point, telling the nurse I had to throw up. She was quite cold and not helpful. She gave me one of those pitiful, tiny kidney-shaped bowls and left, telling me I wasn't going to throw up, that I was fine. (She had obviously never witnessed the velocity with which I can vomit.) The pains were very strong, but the nausea reached a peak. The bathroom seemed a mile away in my current condition.

No compassion.

I felt the waves of nausea and waves of pain escalating as one. Racked with contractions coming within seconds of each other and tangled in the cords, I forced myself out of bed and drug the IV bag with me as I lunged toward the toilet. Tim had fallen asleep, and the nurse certainly wasn't going to help. Moaning in pain with each movement, I made it to the bathroom just in time. In my opinion, some semblance of dignity was salvaged!

In all of this, I continued on — just me and my Lord. He carried me. He was my focal point.

I had spent four months wondering how I would face the end of this journey. *What would God do? Would there be a miracle? Would He save our precious Thomas? Would we be able to endure and withstand this agony?*

In the wee hours of the morning on July 14, 1998, an epidural brought sweet relief and a little rest. God bless the inventor of the epidural! Peace at last!! I rested for a time. When I opened my eyes, Dr. Marcotte was there, looking at me with those familiar eyes of compassion and concern. Tim was sleeping on the couch beside me. The time had come. I was wheeled into a special delivery room with an adjoining room where they work on sick babies. I prayed throughout the pushing.

During our months of waiting to meet Thomas, Dinah used to say, "I can see the grace on you. And, when you get to the end of this journey, His grace will be there, and it will be enough."

When the moment came for me to deliver Thomas, it was clear that God's grace truly was sufficient for us. For the second time, my pregnancy ended without a baby's cry. But Thomas was alive.

Thomas Patrick Gerken was born July 14, 1998 at 7:23 a.m. He weighed four pounds and fourteen ounces. He was sixteen–and-a-half inches long. He had auburn hair and brown eyes.

"He has red hair," said Dr. Marcotte. I twisted to get a glimpse as Thomas was whisked quickly away by a team of experts who worked to keep him alive. I prayed as tears streamed down my face. I was still asking for the miracle of Thomas' life. All those months of wondering what would meet me in the moments of my Thomas' birth, all those questions. The answers washed over me, bringing sweet, unexplainable peace with them. The answer to the ugly question on that first day of his diagnosis, *Where is your God now?* In that moment, I knew of the sufficient grace spoken of in scripture, as it surrounded and carried me. The answer to that question: "Where was my God?" He was right here. He met me there in that place. His grace was waiting. He sustained us, and His presence filled the room.

Jesus was with us, so close that I could feel His presence, as if I could reach out and touch Him. It seemed that time stopped and everything else faded away.

Tim and I were taken back to the recovery room to wait. We were given updates on Thomas' condition a couple times. With prayers still on my lips, I fell asleep, exhausted. Everything was in God's hands. There was nothing we could do — but hope, pray, and wait.

Eventually, we were allowed to see Thomas. Tim chose not to go at first. It was a great struggle for him. Sometimes when our pain is so extreme, we do our best to rest in those protective measures, thinking we can put a wall up to keep the pain out.

The nurse helped me from my bed into a wheelchair and took me to meet our second son. And, when I did, he took my breath away. His beauty was astounding. I was afraid for so long, unsure what I may see when I laid eyes on him. And, I had nothing to fear. He was breath-taking. Perfect. One of the most beautiful babies I have ever seen. I leaned over the little isolette, past all the wires and stroked his cheek. He was hooked up to monitors that beeped and blinked and breathed for him. His little body shuddered with each breath. I asked if he was in pain. The nurse assured me that they would make him comfortable.

I whispered in his ear, "Hello, my baby. Hi, precious. Jesus is with you and I am here. Your Mommy is here. I love you so much."

I kissed his cheek and held his tiny fingers. His eyes were closed, but he was warm and alive.

"You're not alone, Thomas. You're not alone."

I had so much peace; it was surreal. I could only stay a little while before Thomas was in distress again. The machines sustaining his life beeped and blinked with urgency. Alarms went off. The nurse said that his lung was collapsing and I would have to go so they could stabilize him. It was difficult to watch our son struggling, but I knew that he was in God's hands. I felt the Lord's presence blanketing and comforting Thomas … and me.

I went back to another room to wait.

We didn't know about comfort care or birth plans. I knew I wanted time with my son, alive, if possible. I wanted to be his mother on earth, for a little while before having to say goodbye. I knew that I wanted them to make sure that there was nothing that could be done, before we let him go. Potter's Syndrome is fatal, but I wanted them to make sure their diagnosis was correct, that Thomas did not have kidneys, that there was truly no way of sustaining his life. If there was a way, we wanted them to save him.

They came to tell me that we could see Thomas now, but the doctors needed to speak to both of us. They wanted to discuss how to proceed with Thomas' care.

I went to Tim and explained that we both had to be present to talk to the doctors. We sat in a room with several doctors and nurses. They told us that they had determined that Thomas indeed had Potter's Syndrome. He was born without kidneys. His lungs were not able to sustain his life. He was on a respirator, and if kept alive much longer he would be suffering from the lack of kidneys. There was nothing that could be done for him. Even if a kidney transplant was an option, his lungs didn't work well enough on their own to keep him alive. He had other problems as well. We could spend some time with him, but there wasn't a lot of time left before they would have to put him on dialysis to keep him alive. We needed to give them permission to stop the machines soon.

They gave us a couple minutes together. Tim and I held each other and cried.

Before Tim saw Thomas, a nurse sternly spoke to me about his avoidance of the situation, as he stayed in the recovery room, while I was in the NICU.

She said, "You need to convince him to come see this child.

You aren't doing him any favors protecting him."

I didn't have the words to answer her in those fragile moments, sitting next to my son's isolette, spending the only time I would get on planet earth with my child. If I could speak to her now, I would tell her that she wasn't there as we stood beside the grave of our twin baby girls on a cold November day, or while my young husband waited at home, at the tender age of twenty-one wondering if his wife and children would survive. She wasn't there the day when the life disappeared and darkness settled deep as we heard the words "incompatible with life". Or in the months to come while we waited to meet another baby, and to face another tiny grave as we tried to find the grace necessary to say goodbye. I would tell her that she has no right to judge what a man does to survive the inconceivable. We all stumble through the things that are bigger than us, the best we can. And, I would also tell her that I would do almost anything to have been able to protect even one member of my family from this excruciating goodbye. She had no right to judge Tim's performance or mine in those desperate moments.

Tim did meet his son.

I believe it was the same nurse who denied my request to give my son his only bath. I had read in the book Empty Arms that I could bathe my son. I wanted so desperately to mother him, and do the things I would not get to do in the years to come. I told the nurse of my desire to give Thomas a bath once the machines were gone, and he had passed.

She responded, "Oh, no, we will take care of that. That would be just too hard for the parents."

I wasn't strong enough to argue, as our sweet baby's life slipped away. So, I didn't give my son his only bath.

Thomas was alive on this earth for six hours. Although God

did not work the kind of miracle that I asked for, there were miracles that day. Thomas was beautiful! There were no scars on him and his limbs were intact. There was NO evidence that remaining pregnant without amniotic fluid had harmed him (outwardly) in any way!

Tim and I went to see Thomas together before they shut off the machines. The nurses put up a privacy screen in the midst of the NICU. I was allowed to hold our sweet boy for the first time. A nurse handed him to me, and he felt so good to my aching arms. I talked to him and we prayed over him, dedicating him to the Lord. They asked us if we wanted to have Thomas baptized by a Pastor, but we said no. We wanted to dedicate him to the Lord ourselves. Tim sat with us, but he chose not to hold him.

The entire time we were with Thomas, a nurse was taking pictures for us with a disposable camera. As I was holding our sweet baby boy and talking to him, he opened his eyes and looked right at me for just a moment! It was amazing! I actually laughed out loud in awe. Even more incredible – at that very moment – the nurse snapped a picture so that I will always remember that amazing gift. The nurses and doctors who cared for our Thomas that day with such tenderness and dignity left their footprints forever etched upon our hearts.

A nurse led me to a room with a rocking chair. She said she would take Thomas off the machines and bring him to me. She laid him in my arms and I rocked him. At some point, during the last moments of Thomas' life, I began singing and worshipping. As he left this earth, I was filled with peace. The Lord's presence was so strong.

It occurred to me that I had been given a great privilege. I had been chosen to sing to this beautiful baby as he went straight from my arms to the arms of Jesus. I was bathed in peace and an indescribable joy. It was worth a lifetime of being Thomas' mother to be the one who held him and sang to him on his way to heaven. I have never felt closer to Jesus than in that moment. His peaceful presence was so close, it felt like I could almost reach out and touch the hem of His garment as He brushed past me to carry my Thomas home. I knew that He existed in a way that I never had known before. His promises are real, and He will not leave us or forsake us.

I could never have envisioned in my limited human mind that He would have such a blessed, healing experience waiting for me at the end of this journey. I felt that something in me had been restored, even from the loss of our daughters. Somehow, I was even more certain that they were safe in the arms of Jesus. I had been feeling that I had been robbed of the chance to be their mother. But something about the way I was able to say good-bye to Thomas, and feel that peace and even joy, healed what was broken in me.

I was truly blessed among women that day, blessed among Mothers.

"… I will not forget you! See, I have engraved you on
the palms of my hands; your walls are ever before Me."
– Isaiah 49:

Chapter 9
This is the Day the Lord Has Made

Before we left the hospital, I hugged Dr. Marcotte and assured him that God would help us through this. I shared my experience with him. And I was grateful that he wanted to hear about my Thomas. He left with tears in his eyes, forever changed by the life of our son.

Ginny came to the hospital and held Thomas. He was breath-takingly beautiful. And the only outward sign of his affliction was that his pinky toe had grown sideways. I smiled at the thought of it. It was like a special joke between Thomas, God, and us. It still makes me smile.

The time I spent with Thomas (and Jesus) was such a life-changing gift, I was certain that I must have actually glowed for a little while afterwards. When I called from the hospital to tell Dinah the news, it must have surprised her to hear the utter joy in my voice.

"Guess what I just got to do?" I asked breathlessly.

"What?"

"I just got to hold Thomas and sing to him as he went to heaven. I could feel Jesus' presence."

I consider it one of the greatest privileges of my life.

I had struggled through my wilderness, unsure of what I would meet on the other side. Knowing that even in that moment, my Lord would be there to comfort and strengthen me, to grow my meager faith. It is true that His strength is made perfect in our weakness.

I knew that there would be difficult days ahead, but what a reassuring gift I had received to know that my God was and is able to handle ANYTHING. The true miracle isn't as much that He is able, but that He is willing. I would always be able to look back at this day and know who Jesus really is and what His love looks like- when my faith is weak, when I am weary, in the face of the enemy's attack. Nothing could ever take that day from me.

And we know that in all things God works for the good of those who love Him, who have been called according to His purpose.
– Romans 8:28

This time, I knew the grief and doubts ahead. I knew how important it was that I not have any regrets about the way we remembered Thomas' short life on this Earth. I had planned what Thomas would wear at the funeral, what music would be played, and whom I wanted to do the service. I chose our friend and brother in the Lord, Dinah's husband, Dan to speak at the service. I knew that I wanted us to sing "Amazing Grace". We also played a song by Wes King called "Thought You'd Be Here". I was even able to choose the scriptures that I wanted read at the service. God's Word had sustained me so completely throughout this journey. I had truly learned that His Word is living – His truth is freedom and life. Now, the Word would be used again to comfort and sustain us in our time of grief.

He humbled you, causing you to hunger and then feeding you with manna, which neither you nor your fathers had known, to teach you that man does not live on bread alone but on every word that comes from the mouth of the LORD.
– Deuteronomy 8:3

Still protective of our grief and one another, I respected Tim's desire that we keep the funeral private, inviting only a few people. I now wish we would have been able to have more people meet our Thomas. I think they would have a better understanding of our grief and this sweet life that was lost. And, I think they would have been blessed to know him, to meet our precious son. I also wish that we would have allowed Timothy (our son, who was 4 at the time) to be more involved. I wish I would have brought him to the hospital when Thomas was still alive, and included him in the entire funeral. I did bring him to the viewing and allow him to meet Thomas there. Our friends Dan and Dinah were there, along with our mothers and stepfathers, our brothers, and Ginny (the one who walked with me).

Thomas was beautiful … taking our breath away. He was wearing a soft, baby blue outfit I had chosen for him, and his casket was white, lined in blue. He was covered in a white blanket my mother made with her own hands, a cross with a little boy praying, and a little teddy bear dressed in blue.

Ginny and I went to develop the film, which contained Thomas' pictures the day after I left the hospital. It was important to me that we have the pictures for the service. Ginny took the film into WalMart and gave fierce and specific instructions to be extra cautious with the film, telling the technician these were the only pictures I would ever have of my son.

This time I wouldn't leave out any details. I didn't want to miss any opportunity to be his mother. Planning his funeral doesn't seem like much, but it was all I had. There would be no baseball games, no birthday parties, no graduation, no wedding. This funeral was something I could do as his mother and it had to be just right. It turns out that it was more perfect than I could have planned it. You see, Thomas had a mother who loved him dearly, but his heavenly Father's love greatly surpassed even that of his mother. When our heavenly Father plans something, it is better than we could ever hope or imagine!

On the stationary for Thomas' funeral there was a picture of a blue sky with beautiful, billowy clouds. On the front, there was a poem, which read:

> *When God sends forth a tiny soul*
> *To learn the ways of earth,*
> *A mother's love is waiting here*
> *We call this wonder birth.*
> *When God calls home a little soul*
> *And stills a fleeting breath,*
> *A Father's love is waiting there,*
> *This too is birth, not death.*

In Thomas' memory book I wrote about the day of his funeral:

"You were laid to rest beside your sisters Faith and Grace. The day was beautiful. It seemed God made it perfect, just for us. It was just as I wanted it.

Our friend and brother in the Lord, Dan Kruse, spoke and prayed eloquently. We sang and prayed, and praised the Lord for Thomas and one another."

It was July 17, 1998 at 1:30 p.m. The sky was blue with — you guessed it — big, beautiful, billowy clouds. The sun was shining and the breeze was just right. I had wanted to sing a special song on that day, but I wasn't sure if I would be able to do that.

I was able. What grace! Behold what manner of love the Father has lavished on us that we should be called children of God. (I John 3:1) I was unsure if I would have the strength to get the words out on the day of our baby boy's funeral. But, I stood, smiling as the breeze swept passed my cheek and the sun shone on my face. That is the power and love and mercy of the great God I serve.

When I opened my mouth to sing, the words poured out:

When this journey is finally over,
And life's sun sets at last,
Will I find your hand in my hand,
Oh, and all life's sorrow's past.

Just to stand in thy fair city,
With the multitudes unknown.
Is the goal of my heart only,
Just to sit before your throne.
Just to sit before your throne.

I was blessed again that day. I learned what true joy and peace from the Lord felt like. It is different than fleeting happiness or "the peaceful, easy feeling" of this world that comes and goes depending on the circumstances.

John 14:27 says, *Peace I leave with you; my peace I give you. I do not give to you as the world gives. Do not let your hearts be troubled and do not be afraid.*

What gifts I had been given; what freedom. I had faced one of my greatest fears twice, and I knew Who would be there in the fire with me.

*I know what it is to be in need, and I know what it is
to have plenty. I have learned the secret of being content in any
and every situation, whether well fed or hungry, whether living
in plenty or in want. I can do everything through him
(Jesus Christ) who gives me strength.
– Philippians 4:12 &13*

Chapter Ten
The Root of Bitterness

With Thomas, my grief was different. I was so blessed and comforted in the moments I had as Thomas' mother. Still glowing from the presence of Jesus when He carried Thomas home, my heart experienced such healing. It meant so much to me to be the one to hold him as he left this earth. I was shocked by the loss of Faith and Grace, robbed of the chance to mother them. The moments I shared with Thomas healed that broken part of me. I felt assured that my babies were with Jesus, and for several days, I just basked in the glow of that promise.

The days passed and the pain came. I ached for my little one. And the grief beckoned once more. I was rebellious about the grief this time, though. I steadied myself, digging in my heels in resistance when the first waves did indeed rush in a few days after Thomas' funeral. My breasts filled with milk, and again, there was no baby to feed. As if my body were weeping, nothing would stop the flow. But, while my body wept, I did not want to give in to the depth of the sorrow again.

I knew that it could control me, taking me to dark places where the pain is bigger than everything else. I didn't want to give in to it this time. I didn't want to be grief's captive, tossed about at its mercy. I knew the depth of those dark, painful places. I knew if I were carried there again, the pain would be too great. So when the waves of grief came, I refused to be overcome by them. I would start to cry and then fight it off, shaking my head and saying "NO" out loud. I wouldn't go back to that place.

It was not some noble thing, or even some great strength I possessed. It was actually a little cowardice. I just didn't want to hurt that badly again. I remember saying to Ginny when this journey first began:

"I don't want anybody's stinking flowers or sympathy cards this time. I want my baby. If anybody sends me flowers, I will throw them up against the wall and take joy from watching them shatter into a million pieces, just like my broken heart."

So when Ginny was going to send me flowers, she said, "I thought I'd send you something to throw."

That's a true friend.

Unfortunately, in my rebellion against the enemy of grief, I began to use anger as my protective mechanism. Everything around me was shrouded in what I didn't have. I tried to cling to God's promises, remembering what He did for me on in my hour of greatest need. And it did sustain me. But I am still human flesh and envy crept in through the cracks in my faith.

It was difficult to be around someone who was pregnant, joyfully expecting her little one. I found it especially hard to watch large families or to see siblings interacting with one another. Another painful experience was watching expectant fathers experience the joy of waiting for their child to be born, or celebrating that new birth. Baby showers were a nightmare. People seemed to take it for granted that if they were pregnant there would be the birth of a baby to celebrate.

I resented what had been robbed from my family – the joy of pregnancy and childbirth, the certainty of a newborn baby's cry. It drove me crazy if someone talked in such a way that they took this miracle for granted, or complained with a selfish attitude about the slightest inconvenience.

I would say that loathing those who waited with joy for a baby, when they were pregnant, was a good clue that a root of bitterness was springing up inside me. Once again, in my mind, my pain, loss and suffering seemed bigger than almost anything else. I believed God's promises, but I was feeling sorry for myself about what I had lost.

I felt that I was lacking as a woman, that I couldn't give this to my family; that I had brought this sorrow upon us. I still longed for a baby to complete our family and fill our arms and hearts. But, this time, I had to face the reality that it may never happen. It was a good possibility that I would not have another chance at having a baby. I couldn't lean on that hope to ease my pain.

Being driven by anger, bitterness, and envy can consume you. I was a terrible friend to those around me who were expecting. I was lost in my own pain and circumstances. The root of bitterness grew within me, and soon it threatened to choke the life out of my joy. How did I get this way?

Some words from the Walking With You Blog/Threads of Hope Bible Study:

Getting Out of the Pit

I have been in the pit, and through this ministry, I spend a great deal of time with others who are in the pit of grief. And, when you're in the pit, it's tough to think of anything other than the pain and sorrow weighing down on you, being heaped upon you as you sink further in.

Corrie Ten Boom – "There is no pit so deep that God's love is not deeper still."

I love that ... and I could also relate to what Gwen Kik shared:

"After Hope died I felt as if I were hanging in a pit. The only thing keeping me from falling to the depths was my grasp. On the edge of the pit was our Lord, offering His hand but I would not look at Him or reach for Him. I would only hold to the hem of His robe. Some called that faith. I called it desperation. He was all that I had to hold on to."

"I hung there for many months before I had the courage to even look at Him. I remember the day clearly that I climbed out of my pit, into His arms and had a good cry. That was the beginning of my letting go."

When in the pit, we may not have the strength, desire, or will to even reach our hand up to take His ... to even lift our head to look into His eyes, to even open our mouth to whisper ... "help me, hold me, carry me." Even that may be too much. Just breathing is a lot to ask in the smothering depths of the pit.

What I love most about Gwen's picture is that the Lord is sitting outside the pit ... waiting for her ... offering His comfort and reassurance. Even when we can't feel Him, even when we reject Him, He is there, waiting with unyielding love to gather us in His arms and wipe our tears.

I also love that Gwen says she clung to Him out of desperation. I think there's too much emphasis placed on the strength of our faith.

Faith isn't about us. It's about the God we trust in and what He is able to do. It's not about how big or well we believe ... or anything else we do. It's not about having strong faith ... and a faith that barely holds on out of desperation is not considered weak faith. Faith, after all, is just knowing that He is the One to hold on to ... it's trusting in what we do not see. It is the "substance of things hoped for; the evidence of things not seen." Call me crazy, but holding on to the little tiny threads of His robe while grasping in desperation in the pit ... where you cannot see the hope, the light, the promise ... that's the most beautiful faith of all. The dirty, messy, nitty-gritty faith that comes when the world is falling apart and there are no answers.

At least, that's what I learned from my own time in the pit ... Teale shared about the veil ... that in grief, we are covered in a veil. We cannot see the full hope and promises. Scripture talks about the veil as well.

> *This hope we have as an anchor for the soul, both sure and steadfast, and which enters the Presence behind the veil, where the forerunner has entered for us, even Jesus ...*
> *– Hebrews 6:19-20*

I love that ... Jesus went before us ... entered for us ... and in Him, our hope is sure and steadfast. He is the anchor for our soul ...

2 Corinth 3:16 promises: Nevertheless when one turns to the Lord, the veil is taken away.

The study also points out the various emotions displayed by the disciples when Jesus faced death on the cross. They went from disbelief, apathy, anger, fear, desperation, grief, denial … and back to grief.

After His death … the women went to the tomb.

John 20:1-18 tells the story …

> *Mary sat weeping outside the tomb, when the resurrected Jesus approaches her. In her grief, she doesn't recognize Him. She finally recognizes Him when He speaks her name and she turns to Him.*

In the conversation, Jesus asks … "Woman, why are you weeping? Whom are you seeking?"

The study asks for our response to this question. I know the obvious answer would be that most grieving moms are weeping because they long for their sweet babies. But, in reference to standing outside the tomb of Jesus … or sitting in a pit of hopelessness … wondering where the Lord has gone? Are you there in that pit of despair? Does it feel like an empty tomb? Are you wondering where the hope and promise has gone? Are you unable to feel His comfort under the weight of your sorrow? Unable to see His goodness through your veil of pain? Are you wondering if He really is who He says He is?

Perhaps, He is standing right before you … asking whom you are seeking. Perhaps He is just waiting for you to lift your eyes and see Him standing there. That's where I found Him when I lifted my eyes from the pit one day.

I just want to take a minute and say that surrendering to the Lord …

coming to the place when you can reach for His waiting hand and
allow Him to pull you from the pit of despair ... .that is a process.
It happens in time, and for many of you, your grief is very fresh.
Don't think that something is wrong with you because you still feel
the weight of your sorrow and little else. Just know that God loves
you with a relentless love and He will not leave you there. He will
wait for you, as long as it takes. Whether you feel Him, or not ...
He is there.

For me, my time in the pit had to do with where my eyes were looking, what my mind was focused on, and inevitably where my heart followed. I was focused on my circumstances and what I thought I lacked. And, quite frankly, I was grieving and hurting. It didn't take long, in that state of mind, for me to become negative, depressed, and hopeless (and of course angry, bitter, and envious), convinced that life was better for those around me.

Please don't get me wrong. There is a natural part of grieving that includes anger and it's part of the process we work through. Everyone grieves differently, and anger comes out in different ways, but it's usually a part of the process. It is also quite acceptable to want to protect ourselves from circumstances that will trigger pain and emotion, such as baby showers and other baby centered activities. Much grace and tenderness is required. Be gentle with yourself if you are a mother in this time, when wounds are fresh and sorrow is great. There is a point, however when we reach a time of choice, whether to allow our anger to consume us and turn into bitterness or to let it go.

The good news is that God didn't leave me there. (*Because of the LORD's great love we are not consumed, for His compassions never fail. They are new every morning; great is Your faithfulness.*

Lamentations 3:22&23) Over the course of a couple months, God began showing me examples of what happens if we allow bitterness to take root in us. He did this by bringing people who were being destroyed by bitterness across my path. Every time I encountered a person in this state of mind (and hardness of heart), He gently reminded me that I had the potential to become lost in bitterness. I had a choice. I could choose to allow this root of bitterness to grow and choke the life out of me; or I could surrender my pain, my anger, my sorrow, confess my envy and bitterness to Him and allow God to restore me. I listened to the Holy Spirit. I recognized the truth, but I was unsure how to let go of something that had already begun to get its damaging tentacles around my heart.

The next step was to look to the place that had the answers — God's Word.

What does the Bible say about bitterness, anger, and envy?

See to it that no one misses the grace of God and that no bitter root grows up to cause trouble and defile many.
— Hebrews 12:15

My dear brothers, take note of this: everyone should be quick to listen, slow to speak, and slow to become angry, for man's anger does not bring about the righteous life that God desires.
— James 1:19&20

A heart at peace gives life to the body, but envy rots the bones.
— Proverbs 14:30

Wow, these verses were a wake-up call for me! If I stayed in this place of bitterness, life would be pretty grim. There would be no relief or healing, no hope for joy to be restored. My next question was — Now what do I do?

For we are his house, if we hold on to our courage and
the hope of which we boast.
So, as the Holy Spirit says:
"Today, if you hear his voice, do not harden your hearts as you
did in the rebellion, during the time of testing in the desert ..."
– Hebrews 3:6b-8

I remembered how God promises in His word to complete the good work He started in us. I remembered how He grows us, perfecting and establishing our faith, through suffering and hardship. Please do not be mistaken. I am not saying that God sends harsh punishments to correct us. The harmful things, the illnesses, the sorrows are not sent by God. We live in a fallen world where babies die, but He does use the hardships in our lives to grow us and teach us-strengthening us, even in our weakness. God does not wish suffering on His children. He weeps with us like a parent weeps for her child.

My desires remained strong, despite the Lord's encouragement. Tim and I were struggling to make a decision whether to have more children someday. We were considering doing something permanent through surgery to prevent another pregnancy just for peace of mind. We didn't want to go through this agony again. Tim especially wanted to protect our family from suffering through another loss, since he couldn't protect us from what we had already endured. Thinking about not ever having the chance to hope for another child was difficult for me. I wanted a reason to hope. I wanted another chance for the joy of childbirth to be restored to this family.

One day, I sat on the kitchen floor, crying in despair at the thought of lost hope. I was asking God if we would get a chance to have another baby. As I sat there crying and praying, I kept hearing these scriptures in my mind over and over again.

Seek ye first the kingdom of God and His righteousness,
and all these things will be added unto you.
– Matthew 6:33

What does that mean, Lord? Does that mean we will have another child if I seek you first?

Seek ye first the kingdom of God, and His righteousness,
and all these things will be added unto you.

Over and over the verse spoke in my mind, until finally, I stopped asking the questions. I began to sing the song that had that verse in it, again and again, until it made sense. My job was to seek the Lord and His will, not to look at my circumstances. I needed to trust that He would take care of our needs. I needed to trust God and, once again, I needed to fix my eyes on Him, seeking only what God wants for us not what we think is best. I needed to surrender … to lay it all down at His feet. Hadn't He already shown that He is more than able to take care of us in any circumstance?

God had reminded me that my eyes needed to be fixed on Jesus. Once He had my attention again, He also reminded me of all that He had already done for me. I was humbled one day, as I sat crying before the Lord, asking Him to help me learn to seek only Him, trying to give Him all of my cares and disappointments. On my knees, He spoke to my heart. He reminded me of His great love for me. I remembered who Jesus had been to me all my life, how He was always there – how He was there in my darkest hour of need. I thought of all the women who were desperate to be a Mother and had no children at all. I was greatly humbled and convicted of my lack of gratefulness as I thought how blessed I had been to have Timothy, how blessed I was that I should ever be called Mommy, and how undeserving I was of all that God had given me.

I reflected on those whom God had put in my life, those who have loved me and cared for me, like my precious husband and my dear Christian friends and my mother. I went from my knees to my face as I thought of the grace of my Savior who died for me and my ungrateful heart. He was at that very moment still interceding for me, still loving me. It is true that His goodness and mercy lead to repentance. For I was humbled into repentance that day. And as God revealed the error of my ways, He also took my eyes off of my pain and my needs and turned them to Him. I remembered who my God was and what He is able to do, despite my many limitations. I gave my burdens to Him that day, on my face with the sweet surrender washing over me. And He took my pain, sorrow, and even that dreaded root of bitterness away.

For as high as the heavens are above the earth,
so great is His love for those who fear Him; as far as the east is
from the west, so far has He removed our transgressions from us.
As a father has compassion on his children, so the LORD has
compassion on those who fear Him
– Psalm 10311&12

Gratefulness seemed to be a powerful key to unlocking the prison that bitterness holds us in. Gratefulness was my cure for bitterness. Fixing our eyes on Jesus doesn't mean that we won't still struggle with thoughts and doubts. But we have, as I mentioned earlier, some responsibility. I shared earlier, about how faith goes hand in hand with obedience. Once our eyes are on Jesus, we must obey the direction He gives.

Chapter 11
Lord, Restore Our Joy

Weeping may last for a night, but joy comes in the morning.
— Psalm 30:5

I tell you the truth, you will weep and mourn while the world
rejoices. You will grieve, but your grief will be turned to joy.
— John 16:20

So with you: Now is your time of grief, but I will see you again
and you will rejoice, and no one will take away your joy.
— John 16:22

I had a choice between a prison shrouded in bitterness or a freedom bathed in joy. I chose joy, but I didn't fully understand the concept of joy. You see joy is not some fleeting feeling, like happiness or anger. Joy is a constant, blessed assurance. No one and nothing can take our joy. It is that precious hope that we have in the Lord's promises, not in changing circumstances. Our joy is steadfast because our God is steadfast. He doesn't change and He keeps all of His promises.

I had been thinking about the verses in Ecclesiastes 3:1-8:

There is a time for everything, and a season for every activity
under heaven:
A time to be born and a time to die,
A time to plant and a time to uproot,
A time to kill and a time to heal,
A time to tear down and a time to build,
A time to weep and a time to laugh,
A time to mourn and a time to dance,
A time to scatter stones and a time to gather them,
A Time to embrace a time to refrain,
A time to search and a time to give up,
A time to keep and a time to throw away,
A time to tear and a time to mend,
A time to be silent and a time to speak,
A time to love and a time to hate,
A time for war and a time for peace.

I wondered if there could be a season of joy. It seemed we had endured a long season of mourning.

Now that God had replaced my bitterness with a grateful heart, I began to pray that He would restore our joy. I asked Him specifically for a season of joy for our family. This time, I wasn't praying that He would change our circumstances or give us another baby, or make everything perfect. I just asked that joy would return to our household.

And He answered that prayer. Our family started to experience a great, healing bond of joy. We had walked through sorrow together. Now we laughed again together. It is important that I communicate that God restored our joy right there, where we were, without changing our circumstances. I still sat in the church pew alone with Timothy on Sunday mornings.

We had still lost three out of four of our children. We still had no earthly hope or plans to ever have another child, but we felt so blessed at what we did have. I could honestly say that our cup overflowed with blessings. We began to experience that abundant life.

When I would share the story of our Faith, Grace, and Thomas with others, the joy and healing of the Lord was always evident. Other people have testified that as they listened to the story of how God carried us through, they could see the grace and healing He had given me. There was no hopelessness in the story. It is a story of how God is not bound by circumstances. He will stand with you in the fire, and He will make sure that you don't get burned. It is a story of His great love for us, His mercy, His grace, and His healing power. It reveals that He is a personal Savior, who will never forsake us.

In that time and place, I felt that joy had been restored. God had given us more than enough. He had sent Jesus to save us. He had given us one another. And He had given us a beautiful son that we dearly loved. He had sustained us in our time of need. And He had restored and strengthened the love and bond of our family. We lacked for nothing. Together the three of us were content to walk on, laughing and living, as a complete family, just as we were. It was more than enough.

If our story ended there, we would truly be a family God had miraculously sustained and healed; more than that He gave us joy. But that was only the beginning of the restoration.

God had whispered a promise to my heart as I surveyed the damage left behind by the loss of our children and the other scars we bore on our hearts from prior wounds that come from living life on this imperfect Earth.

*So I will restore to you the years that the swarming locust
has eaten, The crawling locust, The consuming locust, And the
chewing locust, My great army which I sent among you.*
– Joel 2:25

And, He did … and He still is … restoring the years the locusts have eaten. But He isn't finished. He constantly works to restore the broken places in the quiet depths of our hearts and minds. Places sometimes hidden even to ourselves. I sense that in all the miraculous restoration I have witnessed in my life and the lives of those around me, He has just begun to work His intricate plan. He has just begun to right the wrongs, to heal and restore, to reveal the depth of His love … His plans … His promises for our lives. He has only just begun.

Chapter Twelve
Refining Fire

Though the fig tree does not bud and
there are no grapes on the vines,
Though the olive crop fails and the fields produce no food,
Though there are no sheep in the pen and no cattle in the stalls,
Yet I will rejoice in the LORD,
I will be joyful in God my Savior.
The Sovereign LORD is my strength;
He makes my feet like the feet of a deer,
He enables me to go on the heights.
– Habakkuk 3:17-19

We continued in our journey of healing, and went about the task of living life, content. Timothy started attending school. I worked at his preschool, and now that he was in Kindergarten, I took a job working as a teacher's aide at his elementary school. Tim was working as hard as ever at his job as a foreman in concrete and excavating.

We had just returned from a weekend getaway with my friend Nicki and her husband. A couple of weeks had passed since that fun weekend we spent camping and laughing, enjoying alone time, when I began feeling strange. A small part of me wondered if I might be pregnant again. No, that was impossible, I thought. *I am taking birth control pills. Could this be Lord?*

Time went by and my "monthly visitor" did not arrive. I decided to take a pregnancy test. Actually, I took four, just to make sure! I was astonished to see that little pink line form in the window. Again and again, I saw it. The line that said we were about to embark on this blessed, and for us, treacherous, journey once more.

From the beginning of this pregnancy, I had purposed in my heart to allow myself to have hope. I knew this might be our last chance to have another child. It was a chance we thought we might never have again. We had put it out of our minds. Now that we were blessed with this chance, I decided I wasn't going to let anything, especially my own fears, rob me of this joy.

Tim felt differently about the situation. He was incredibly apprehensive about another pregnancy — and with good reason. It wasn't the thought of another child that was frightening; it was the thought of another loss. He wanted to protect our family from facing that pain once more. Now we were in a situation that seemed risky to him after all we had endured, and he felt uneasy about being in this precarious position again. He was quiet and surprised by the news of the pregnancy. He hugged me, and begrudgingly mustered a doubtful, "It will be O.K." as he stood with a dazed look on his face.

Timothy was very hopeful and prayed with me about the health of this child. Often his sweet six-year-old prayers tugged at my heart as he would say, "Please let this baby stay." I guess we all were protecting our fragile hearts in some way.

It was a battle for me to choose hope and joy when my instincts were to protect myself from the devastation that loss would bring. Stubbornness, more than anything, motivated my devotion to joy. You see, I had been angry that our family was robbed of the joys of pregnancy, and this time, I didn't want to be robbed, spending every moment in fear. Maybe there wasn't anything to fear. God had sent this blessing. We should receive it.

There were tense moments in our household during the days of waiting. Pregnancy had become such an object of pain for us as a couple, and just my existence in this state was an agonizing reminder to Tim of all that we had lost. He began to withdraw from me, working late hours, talking to me less. One day when I was pressing him to communicate with me, he told me that he didn't know if he wanted to be married anymore, and he wasn't sure if he loved me. Then he left for work.

I stood in our bedroom, feeling shattered and shocked. My world had exploded. I felt stripped to the core of my soul, as if left standing naked without my blanket of protection, and robbed of my identity at that moment. But, there wasn't time to dwell too long because Timothy needed to go to school, and I had to go to work. So after being ill and crying for a couple minutes, I went through the motions of the day. I picked myself up and did the next thing.

Tim rarely came home for the next couple months. He retreated from me, communicating only when necessary about our son or bank transactions. I was plagued with nausea, as usual, during the beginning of my pregnancy. But this situation intensified matters. I was vomiting often, at home, at work, everywhere; but that was nothing compared to the hollow pain deep inside of me, gnawing constantly.

I had longed so desperately for another baby to complete our family. And now it seemed that there may not be a family anymore at all. Was I not allowed to want both? Had I been selfish?

Sometimes I thought that there may be an easy way out. Were we supposed to just end our marriage, or continue in this limbo? God would answer my question, but He didn't always answer it the way that I wanted. Every time I grew weary of the endless nights of wondering, asking God if I was allowed to give up hope, He answered. His answer was the same each time: "No, wait, stay, remain; abide in Me." How did I listen when I wanted to flee and God said to stay?

In those moments, three things kept me in obedience. One: I wanted to know that I was obedient to the Lord. I would rather not look back and see that I chose to serve anything or anyone but God. Two: The face of my son and the thought of this family and how much our children needed us to stay. Three: At the twilight of our lives, I wanted to be sitting on the back porch with this man, looking back on the years and know that we stayed – that when life was difficult, we remained faithful. We didn't compromise. I wanted no regrets on my back porch. I wanted to sit there, sipping lemonade with only our family memories between us.

I wasn't very strong. But I was willing. So when God spoke, I listened because I knew I couldn't handle this myself. I needed Him. In my agony, He reminded me — *His grace is sufficient. His strength is made perfect in our weakness.* I desperately searched His word, and this is what I found:

"Do not be afraid; you will not suffer shame.
Do not fear disgrace; you will not be humiliated You
will forget the shame of your youth and remember
no more the reproach of your widowhood.
For your Maker is your husband – the LORD Almighty
is His name – the Holy One of Israel is your Redeemer;

he is called the God of all the earth.
The Lord will call you back as if you were a
wife deserted and distressed in spirit — a wife who married
young, only to be rejected," says your God.
"For a brief moment I abandoned you, but with
deep compassion I will bring you back. In a surge of anger
I hid my face from you for a moment,
but with everlasting kindness I will have compassion on you,"
says the LORD your Redeemer.
– Isaiah 54:4-8

The preceding verses became my new blanket of protection. God was all that I needed. I had nothing to fear. He would keep me from shame, disgrace and humiliation. He is my Maker, my Redeemer. He is the God of all the earth. And I, being a member of His church body am called the bride of Christ. He is all that I need. With everlasting kindness, He will have compassion on me. What a comfort. The most amazing thing about God's Word is how specifically God speaks to our hearts to meet our needs and to teach us His ways. One other special aspect of these verses in Isaiah was how the Lord speaks about a "wife deserted and distressed in spirit, a wife who married young, only to be rejected." He knows the pain of that type of rejection. He understands and cares enough to mention it in His Word. It completely humbles me to realize that He cares and recognizes our pain. This perfect all- knowing, all-powerful, holy and righteous God – the God of the universe cares about our pain, our losses, our sorrow, and our broken hearts.

How precious concerning me are your thoughts, O God! How vast
is the sum of them!

Were I to count them, they would outnumber the grains of sand.
When I awake, I am still with you.
– Psalm 139:17-18

It is a comfort to know that God can fulfill my needs for protection and love. My Maker is my husband – the Lord Almighty is His name. *But what about Timothy and the child growing in my womb?* What will become of them Lord? Is God big enough to take care of them? Yes, but will He?

All your sons will be taught by the LORD, and great will be
your children's peace. In righteousness you will be established:
Tyranny will be far from you; you will have nothing to fear.
Terror will be far removed; it will not come near you.
If anyone does attack you, it will not be my doing; whoever
attacks you will surrender to you.
– Isaiah 54:13-15

… no weapon forged against you will prevail,
and you will refute every tongue that accuses you.
– Isaiah 54:17a

What a specific promise to take care of my family! So, God showed me that my identity was in Him. I could look to Him to meet not only my needs, but also the needs of my family. What about the question of my value and worth? Did my value lie completely in the opinion of my husband?

With one verse God dispelled that false idea:

… many people saw the miraculous signs He (Jesus) was doing
and believed in his name. But Jesus would not entrust himself

to them, for He knew all men. He did not need man's testimony
about man for He knew what was in a man.
– John 2:23b-25

I felt so free! My entire life I struggled with fear of abandonment and feelings of unworthiness. It didn't matter what anyone said or felt about me. It only mattered what God thought. I was still His child and nothing could shake my identity in Him. Nothing could take the value and worth Jesus had placed in me the day He was nailed to a cross and died for every flaw and sin that marred me. I was already "enough" because the blood of Jesus had made me a righteous and beloved child of God. I had nothing to prove to anyone. We should look to Jesus, "the author and finisher of our faith." What did He think of the opinions and testimonies of man? Not much!

It's very common for couples to grieve differently, and marriage has a high rate of failure after the loss of a child. So many emotions build and can come between a husband and wife. She may be able to cry freely and need to talk about the baby and her sorrow. He may want to go to work and focus on something else … anything other than the pain. He may feel overwhelmed by all of her feelings, unable to fix it and make it better, unable to comfort her and protect her from such terrible pain.

It's also not uncommon to feel disillusioned spiritually. Some people feel rejected and forsaken by God. Some people question God and wonder why He allows such pain and loss. Some people turn their back on God, or grow angry and defiant. They may wonder, "How could a loving God allow a little baby to suffer and die?" I felt rejected; Tim just wanted to run as far as possible from all of it.

Yes, we walked this journey together, but we both chose to walk the path so differently. It helped me to remember our children by attending memorial services and talking about their short lives. I was free to express my feelings. Tim grieved his own quiet way, and I respected that. **I think it is essential for couples to realize that everyone grieves differently. Even if one is quiet, his pain is real and the love he felt for the one they lost is real.** Because we respected one another in our grief, I thought that maybe we were safe from the statistics.

What I hadn't thought of though, was the effect another pregnancy may have on the grief that Tim had carefully stored away and protected. I hadn't thought about how all those years running from the sorrow and from God had affected Tim. For years, there were constant obstacles for us to overcome as a family. He directed his unhappiness at our marriage, and me, so it seemed personal and felt personal. Some of it was personal.

We continued on this way for weeks with our marriage in limbo. Close to 12 weeks into the pregnancy, I awoke in the middle of the night to find that I was bleeding. I was upset, but some protective part of me must have been prepared because it didn't seem shocking to me that I could lose the baby. Still, I cried out, "NO!"

My mother drove me to the hospital …

When we arrived, the doctor performed an ultrasound to check the status of the baby. As I lay on the table, I fully expected the resident to look at me and say, "I'm sorry."

She didn't. She looked at me and said the baby was still living, but it looked like part of the placenta may be torn away. She wasn't exactly sure. She said I should go home. I insisted that she schedule an appointment for me to see the doctor first thing in the morning to determine what exactly was happening to my baby. It was four in the morning, and she didn't look very excited about calling Dr. Marcotte at such a late/early hour. She agreed, after realizing there was no changing my mind, and we went home.

The next day I went to Dr. Marcotte's office. He said the bleeding was caused by a subchorion hemotoma. It could repair itself or I could miscarry. At the time, the pregnancy had about a fifty- fifty chance. Even if the hemotoma resolved itself, there was a possibility of preterm labor and other complications later in pregnancy.

We would have to wait and monitor the situation. I was still losing blood, and he mentioned that I might continue to lose some blood for a while. This was not much of a comfort to me — a mother who was already struggling to have hope that this pregnancy may end well.

Here we were again, facing a situation that we had no control over. There was nothing that I could physically do to influence the outcome of this pregnancy or our marriage. I prayed and read everything I could about the problem. I took six weeks off work as a precaution.

Tim did not seem surprised that something was wrong with the pregnancy. Because of all we had been through, he just didn't expect that this would turn out O.K. with a bouncing healthy baby in our arms. He had given up hope. Maybe I was crazy, but I needed to hope. It was all I had.

We continued to struggle separately in our marriage; now with an added twist of stress, for several months. The bleeding stopped eventually. I did not miscarry our baby at that point, and the tear resolved itself. An ultrasound was performed at about twenty weeks of pregnancy, showing no sign of birth defects and also revealed that we would have a son. I was comforted by the fact that our baby looked healthy, but I knew that I wouldn't fully believe we would have another child until I felt him breathing against me in my arms and heard his sweet first cries. Still, I prayed, trusted, and hoped.

I wondered what would happen to our family. Would we ever be restored? I knew God would take care of us, but I didn't want to see my family torn apart by divorce. I knew that God didn't either. After reading Love Must Be Tough by Dr. James Dobson for the third time, I realized that our family couldn't continue in this destructive limbo any longer. I talked to Tim, and we agreed to attend counseling.

Chapter Thirteen
Restoration

He has sent me to bind up the brokenhearted,
to proclaim freedom for the captives and release from darkness
for the prisoners,
To proclaim the year of the LORD's favor and
the day of vengeance of our God,
To comfort all who mourn, and provide for those
who grieve in Zion,
To bestow on them a crown of beauty instead of ashes,
the oil of gladness instead of mourning, and a garment of praise
instead of a spirit of despair.
– Isaiah 61:1b-3

I went to see the counselor myself, speaking with her a few times before Tim and I went together. She was a precious, gentle woman to whom you could tell anything, and not receive judgment in return. She became our counselor and our friend. Sometimes Tim and I wouldn't have spoken to each other all week- not one word. Then we would drive an hour to see her. There we would talk to her. We didn't fight with each other. After we left her office, we would ride home, often in silence. It seemed fitting that the song "Desparado" played on the radio on our trip to and from the counselor.

As time went on, we began to melt a little toward one another. As we often had throughout our marriage, we used humor to diffuse some of the tension between us. Sarcastic humor at times, but humor nonetheless. He started coming home earlier. My pregnancy was nearing an end. Soon life would be changing. I began to let myself think that it was possible that we may actually have a baby. Either way, our son needed a name. We decided to name him James Henry after our grandfathers and Tim's great-grandfather.

In my determination to have hope, Ginny, Dinah, and I planned a baby shower. And we celebrated as I opened gift after gift and marveled at God's ability to make all things new. I didn't want to miss a moment of joy. I wanted pregnancy to mean joy again for us, even in the midst of our misery. It was something that I needed to be redeemed, something that part of me craved so much that I couldn't ignore it. So I received the gifts with gratefulness and hope in my heart, putting away the feelings of fear. I needed to choose joy, no matter what was about to happen to our family. Would there be a death or a birth of a baby? Would there be a death of a marriage or a restoration of a marriage? The answers would come soon enough.

From Sweet Baby James on the Sufficient Grace Blog:

On a sunny day in May, our sweet baby James was born after a grueling labor and a lot of pushing. I didn't hear the cry at first. The cry I had longed to hear for several years.

"Make him cry, Dr. Marcotte.... I don't hear a cry!" Familiar panic tightened around my throat and squeezed my palpitating heart.

And then ... it came, filling the room with it's glory, surrounding me like a healing balm. The sweetest sound on this earth ... the sound of a newborn baby cry … the sound of new life … my baby … my sweet, sweet baby … alive and crying in my arms. Tim looked stunned as James was placed in his arms. "Stunned" soon gave way to joy. We had a baby boy! A boy who had come to stay! Timothy came to the hospital later that evening, and held his brother. Finally, he would not be denied. This baby would be coming home with us to stay … to complete our family.

We each held him and looked at him, in awe and disbelief.
We shed tears — of amazement, joy, gratefulness,
and sorrow for what had been.
Weeping may last for a night, but joy comes in the morning.
– Psalm 30:5

Morning had finally come, and joy had returned to our house once more! Our arms were full, but our hearts swelled to the brim. I happily nursed James and held him against me. We were surrounded by our family who once walked with us through our grief and now stood by us in our happiness. Ginny and Dinah were there, as well, to meet the one who came to stay and brought the gift of joy.

From *The Beauty of Sufficient Grace* blog:
Several months ago, I was tucking James into bed and reading from his children's bible. The bible story shared a miracle. Sadly, I cannot remember the exact miracle, but I do remember our conversation. We were praying for healing for a sick baby and comfort for grieving moms.

James said, "Mom, that was back in the bible time. Jesus doesn't do miracles like that anymore."

"Oh, really?" I replied with raised eyebrows. "I'm looking at a real live miracle right now!"

"What do you mean, Mom?"

"Well, when you were growing in my tummy, you were very sick."

"Like Faith, and Grace and Thomas??"

"Well, kind of. Timothy and Daddy and Mommy prayed for a baby to come to our house and stay. Faith, Grace, and Thomas went to heaven and we were very sad because we missed them. And then came you. But the doctors found a little tear near the placenta ... the part that feeds the baby while he's in the mommy's tummy. And the doctors said that there was a 50% chance that you may not live."

"Really?"

"Yes ... and we waited and prayed. God healed you ... and you are here today. So, Mr. James ... God still definitely does miracles. I'm looking at one. It's you!"

"Wow ... I guess He does still does do miracles." He smiled and sat a little taller. "He let me stay!" He grinned.

God's miracles come in all shapes and sizes. Sometimes God calms the storm ... sometimes He quiets us with peace. Sometimes He gives physical healing on this earth ... sometimes He heals by taking a soul to heaven - the ultimate, complete, and permanent healing. They are all miracles. The teenager that grows as we speak (blog) made us parents and is truly a miracle. The three sweet babies who spend their days dancing in heaven are most certainly valued miracles whose lives have touched thousands, and whose lives were used to draw us closer to the Lord and show us more of who He is. And, sweet baby James, who beat the odds and was "allowed to stay" (as both boys have said) with us is most certainly a miracle. But none is more precious or valued than the other. We know that we don't always get the earthly miracle. We know that … and when we don't, His grace is sufficient to carry us … and even that … even the beauty that comes from such hideous ashes … the beauty of a changed heart, a changed life … is truly a miracle, indeed. Maybe the most beautiful miracle of all …

As the days passed, our exuberance grew even stronger. We began to communicate in our marriage as never before. There were times when I struggled with the words that had been spoken in that difficult time. But Tim was able to communicate with me that he had really been struggling with the loss of our children and all the painful feelings, memories, and fears another pregnancy brought to the surface. It wasn't really only about our marriage or me. He didn't want more pain for our family. He feared another loss. He just wanted to run away from all of it. But now, something had been healed that once was broken and we had been restored in more ways than one.

God doesn't just restore what is taken from us; He makes all things new. He makes it even better than it was. He can make beauty from ashes, and that is what He did in us. We had done everything to set ourselves up for failure. Every statistic was against us in our marriage, but that didn't matter to God. He's not concerned with circumstances or statistics. We had gone into the fiery furnace, but we were never alone. We faced the refining fire with our Savior by our side. When He redeems what is lost and heals what is broken He does it perfectly and better than anything we can think of or imagine in our own power. God's healing and restoration is complete. He wants us to lack nothing.

The healing and restoration of our family began before we had James, and at his birth our cup overflowed. But God wasn't finished yet. Tim and I faced the path to forgiveness for the months of strain our marriage had endured. We were blessed with two beautiful children on this earth and three in heaven, and somehow we still had one another. Gratefulness was a familiar cure for some of our pain. We were grateful that we had another chance. God had always taken care of us. Even though some parts of our marriage still needed healing, He could see us through. And He did.

We learned about the power of forgiveness. We were taught the love does not keep a record of wrongs. Perfect love drives out fear. We can and should forgive because we are forgiven. Our God is merciful, giving us His grace and forgiveness in the place of punishment and justice.

There was a moment, when I was struggling with the wounds, still raw from that season of turmoil between us. Forgiveness is such a pretty word, like grace and faith. Sometimes we forget the nitty, gritty, dirty parts of the actual laying down and surrendering necessary to forgive. It is the ultimate "dying to self," laying down your right to "keep a record of wrongs," releasing the guilty party and wiping the debt-filled slate clean. Tim's momentary abandonment, at least emotionally in our marriage was a betrayal to me. Leaving or being left is my kryptonite. Once I knew our family would survive, I was hurt and angry. So many tattered pieces were left to sort through, and yet, life continued.

One day, in a tense prayer/conversation with God, I was

pouring out the hurts, laying them at His feet. *I don't know how to forgive him for doing this. How do I trust? How do I give my heart? He hurt me.*

He whispered to my heart, *What would make it better? How can he make it right?*

I tearfully replied, *He can't. The only way it will ever be right is if it never happened at all.*

The Lord left me to chew on my own words awhile. I realized it was impossible for Tim, to go back in time and make it right. And, he was here now, doing his best to make today right and the future. Immediately, I was reminded of all the grace that had been afforded to me, all the wrongs I had been forgiven in this life. Who was I not to forgive the man I married?

I wish I could explain exactly how God helped us to heal and forgive, or at what point our marriage had been restored. The best I can describe is the analogy given earlier about the leaves and the trees. How subtly God works in us to change and heal until one day what once was is no more. One day, we realize that He has taken our sorrow, our baggage, our failure, our pain, our sin – whatever weight has been hindering us and turned it into a blessing rather than a burden. Where once there was sin, now there is forgiveness. Where sorrow once lived, now joy dwells. Where once there was death, now there is life. Once the trees were barren. Now they spring forth green leaves and beautiful, life-giving fruit.

I don't know exactly when or how He took the tattered ashes of our lives and made them into something beautiful; but one day, all the pain was gone. One day, there was nothing left to forgive. One day love prevailed. In reality, though it wasn't one day. It had been happening all along. God had been using every circumstance, every tear, every moment of brokenness to make beauty from ashes, to turn our shame into a crown of glory, to heal our pain and restore us, turning our deepest sorrow into our most exuberant joy.

Throughout this journey, each time we walked through a fiery trial, there were choices to be made. Sometimes we may not see clearly in those agonizing moments. It can feel like we are standing on the edge of a cliff in thick fog. But if we are seeking the Lord as we stand on that cliff, we are not alone. And if we listen to His voice when He answers our cry, just obey — take the next step, He will catch us. He will give us the grace we need to walk on this sacred ground, trusting Him when we don't see. Some choices can be deceiving. One way might seem easier than another. But God's ways are always best. He is always right there and all we have to do is take His hand and allow Him to lead us through the foggy times. (Maybe it isn't fog as much as smoke from the refining fire in our trial!)

We all have choices along the way. Each day, we have a choice about how we will respond in various situations, sometimes even extremely difficult circumstances. When we have an opportunity to be used by God in someone else's life, we have a choice. Throughout this story, I have mentioned some of the people along the way who took the time, or recognized an opportunity to make a difference in our lives. Maybe they listened or showed concern. Maybe they sat by our side or gave us a bible verse. Maybe they sent food to our family or a card or gift. Maybe they said a prayer or shed a tear. It was our friends, our teachers, our doctors, our nurses, and the stranger at Meijer … God uses us wherever we are. I have a plaque in my garden that says "Bloom Where God Plants You." We all have opportunities to be used; we have choices in our own lives and we have choices in how we respond to others. We all have opportunities to leave our footprints etched on the hearts of others.

As we walk through our lives with our Lord, He teaches us about who He is and about His great love for us. He teaches us to trust Him by allowing us to be in a situation where we see our great weakness and need for Him. We trust Him because when we are in that situation, He is there and He carries us through. Each time we choose to follow Him in the midst of our trials, He shows more of who He is. As we look back on all that He has done, that's how our faith grows. We remember that He does not leave us. He keeps His promises. We know because we lived it; we walked it; and we never walked alone.

One thing God had taught me about faith was that my faith does not rest in whether we will be asked to walk through the fire again. But my faith rests in the knowledge that when the fiery trials come, as I said before, my Savior is there in the midst of the fire. And when we are on the other side of that trial we know that the joy that awaits us will make every moment worthwhile.

I also learned the great beauty of God's grace in our lives. His transforming power amazes me as He takes imperfect jars of clay with all of our broken scarred pieces and molds us into beautiful vases. He has redeemed what my sin had destroyed. He is strong when I am weak. When I am faithless, He is faithful. He does make beauty from ashes. My entire life is an example. For nothing good dwells in me apart from Him. He saved me and is transforming me day-by-day, promising to finish the good work He started in me. Everyday I look at this family and stand in awe of my God's restoring, healing power. And the truly incredible thing isn't that He can work in us to change and restore, but that in His great mercy (which I cannot comprehend) *He is willing.*

Yet the LORD longs to be gracious to you;
He rises to show you compassion.
For the LORD is a God of justice.
Blessed are all who wait for Him!
– Isaiah 30:18

Another thing God taught me through this journey was the meaning of love. True love does not have conditions. It isn't dependent on what the other person can do for you. It isn't a feeling that comes and goes. True love is a choice. It's a choice to believe when circumstances tell you to doubt. It's a choice to stay when it looks like you should flee. It's a choice to keep going when you want to give up. True love gives when there's nothing left to give. It's dying to your self, giving up your right to whatever feeling you have at that moment, whatever right you think you're due. It's impossible for human beings to express or even know true love without the Holy Spirit.

Love is patient, love is kind. It does not envy, it does not boast,
it is not proud. It is not rude, it is not self-seeking, it is not easily
angered, it keeps no record of wrongs. Love does not delight in
evil but rejoices with the truth. It always protects, always trusts,
always hopes, always perseveres. Love never fails …
– I Corinthians 13:4-8a

This is how we know what love is: Jesus Christ laid down his life
for us. And we ought to lay down our lives for our brothers.
– I John 3:16

Dear children, let us not love with words or tongue but with
actions and in truth. – I John 3:18

There is no fear in love. But perfect love drives out fear …
— I John 4:18a

We began our story with two teenagers searching for love in all the wrong places. As this story ends, the search is over but the real story is just beginning. You see, through this difficult journey, we learned that "true love" exists in the love our Heavenly Father has for us. He loves us and fills us with that same enduring love for one another.

During our pregnancies, my friend Ginny would often accompany me to appointments.

Dr. Marcotte would say, "Where is Tim? How is he doing?"

I would respond, "He's working and doing a lot of fishing."

Tim spent a lot of time coping by immersing himself in busyness and the solitude offered by nature. For many years, I went to church alone, praying for Tim, learning to accept and love him whether or not he shared my abiding faith. God taught me how to do that, how to honor my husband and how to have an abundant, unequally yoked marriage, full of love. I would have accepted it as enough. But, God wanted more for us.

Shortly after James's birth, God whispered to my heart that Tim would one day share the church pew with us, completing our family. He spoke to my heart that when it happened, it would be as if he had been there all along, worshiping together with us, loving and serving the Lord. Oh, how I longed to look down and see Tim's hands folded in prayer alongside mine and the tiny hands of our sweet boys. How I longed for our family picture to be complete on Sunday mornings, for his presence to fill the void in the church pew.

God reminded me of a promise He had given me in the early years of our marriage. He didn't want us to just have a partial healing, to walk but with a limp. He wanted us to be complete, fully restored in Him. I began to pray for Tim, as the Lord impressed upon me that He was already preparing Tim's heart to fully receive Him. When he went fishing, God would whisper to me, "I will make you fishers of men." Tim would come home and share a story about helping someone in need while he was out on his boat or spending some time with a child that lacked a fatherly influence, teaching another how to fish. I would smile, knowing that God was already at work.

When Tim would sit in the woods for hours on end, waiting to shoot that elusive deer, God spoke to my heart:

There is no where he can go where I cannot speak to him. Pray that no matter where he is, he would feel My presence, that he would hunger and thirst for My righteousness. If he is in a tree stand, pray that I would speak to his heart in the silence, through the beauty of My creation.

So, I quietly prayed, unbeknownst to Tim. I prayed that God would meet him wherever he was. God loved Tim through me, and I kept praying. One day, as Mother's Day approached, I felt prompted to ask Tim for a special gift. I asked him to go to church with us.

And … he did.

He didn't come every Sunday at first, but the teaching of the Word had pricked his heart and slowly chipped away at the shell he had built around it. Soon, he was there in the pew, every Sunday, and I smiled as I looked over at little James to see him folding his own hands in prayer as he followed Daddy's lead. My eyes lingered on those calloused hands, rough from hard work, rough from the grit of life, folded in prayer with little eyes looking on. I blinked back the tears as I remembered God's promise.

It is true, that it was as if he had always been there. James does not even know there was ever a time when Tim wasn't there. So natural was Tim's yielding to the Lord. Soon, he was playing his guitar while I lifted my voice to sing during children's worship and later junior worship, occasionally in the sanctuary, and now as we visit various churches with our Christian praise band, One Way. He humbly leads by his quiet example. God literally has allowed us to reap with *songs of joy*. And, it continues to be one of the most precious, astounding gifts of my life.

Tim allows his life to speak much more than his words, and we don't have many deep conversations about what transpired during those years. Several years after Tim began attending church, we were in a bible study, sharing our testimonies of how we came to know Jesus. Tim tentatively began to answer when I asked him to share. What he said left us both weeping.

Without ever knowing what God had whispered to my heart, or all the prayers I prayed for him, Tim began to share that when he was fishing or sitting in the tree stand, he knew God was with him, and that he always felt peace as he spent time admiring God's creation. He also mentioned that I never gave up on him.

I couldn't believe the beautiful miracle of how God met him in those woods and how he so specifically whispered to my heart to pray for Tim. I wept openly as I shared those prayers with him for the first time in the middle of the bible study, where others began to speak of their own prayers for Tim over the years. Love surrounded us. I was in awe of the greatness of God's love for us, astounded at the miracle that He pursued Tim, even when he hid in the woods. And, He pursued me, and kept me … kept us both, with his relentless love.

Today, because of that love, my family walks hand in hand along life's precious journey together toward the twilight of our lives- toward our back porch where we will sip lemonade with only the memories between us, toward our heavenly home where all will be perfected and completely restored. Then, we will be reunited with our children who have gone to Heaven before us and I pray we will hear the only sound sweeter than a newborn baby's cry: the voice of our Beloved saying, "Well done, My good and faithful servant."

Our mouths were filled with laughter, our tongues with
songs of joy. Then it was said among the nations,
"The LORD has done great things for them."
The LORD has done great things for us,
And we are filled with joy.
Restore our fortunes, O LORD like streams in the Negev.
Those who sow in tears will reap with songs of joy.
— Psalm 126:2-5

Part Two:
SUFFICIENT GRACE MINISTRIES

Chapter Fourteen
Comforting Others With the Comfort We have Received ...

In 1996 when we met and said goodbye to our Faith and Grace and in 1998 when we met and said good-bye to our Thomas Patrick, things were much different than they are today. When Faith and Grace were born, we held them briefly while I sang "Amazing Grace" and said a prayer. The nurses took our baby girls and shot some poor quality Polaroids (although we do appreciate their attempts). We were given a little quilted pink bundle with their tiny preemie diapers, the Polaroids, the book Empty Arms and sent on our not-so-merry way.

When we received the fatal diagnosis of Potter's Syndrome midway through our pregnancy with Thomas, we heard the words "incompatible with life" for the first time and we were also sent on our grief stricken, forsaken-feeling, heart-broken way. To make a choice. An impossible choice.

It was before.

Before organizations like Be Not Afraid ...

Before perinatal hospice ...

Before Now I Lay Me Down to Sleep ...

Before we were inspired by the journeys of so many other bloggers who courageously clung to the Lord and His promises in the midst of the storm as He held them in the grip of His grace ...

It was before I even had a computer!

We were still on the outskirts of a time when parents quietly grieved as the world moved on. We did continue our pregnancy with Thomas, but we didn't have a maternity Now I Lay Me Down to Sleep photo shoot. We didn't feel that we could embrace and fully cherish our time with Thomas with the outside world, at least. I treasured the time in the quiet of my heart.

We felt weak, often just clinging to the Lord to get through. I didn't have a birth plan … didn't know there was such a thing. I didn't know anyone else who chose to continue their pregnancy after a fatal diagnosis, and some in the medical profession thought we were crazy for doing so. (Not my wonderful, compassionate maternal fetal medicine physician, Dr. Marcotte, but some.)

Although, carrying Thomas was one of the greatest privileges of my life, it was lonely, navigating through those uncharted waters, carrying a baby with a fatal diagnosis to term, with little support and virtually no guidance. Some support exists for families who walk this path today, but we were not afforded such opportunities.

We had a quiet, private service for our babies when they passed. And, people didn't know what to say, how to comfort us, how to support us. We carried our babies and our grief in silence, not displaying pictures … not sharing the lives of our sweet children with the world. We were quiet as we were carried through the relentless waves of grief, sharing it with only those closest to us, rarely discussing it with one another. At the time, we were just trying to survive. I didn't have the voice to share our journey for many years. But, in 2004, God began to awaken my heart to share Faith and Grace and Thomas with others … to reach out to offer comfort and hope. And, He gave me a voice.

Sufficient Grace Ministries for Women (and families) was born.

I am so grateful for the support and inspiration we have today from the organizations I listed above and from the brave mothers and families who have shared their babies with the world. That we may all have a voice. Mothers who walk this journey will know that they don't walk alone. Because of their courage, their faith, because of God's unbelievable grace … the families who walk this path today can know that others have walked before them … .cherishing the gift of life, no matter how brief. The message that every life matters, every life holds purpose and value … that message gives other moms the courage to trust God to carry them and their babies with His sufficient grace. I'm so thankful to all of those courageously lending their voices to tell their stories … to tell His story.

The Birth of the Dreams of You Memory Book and the Comfort Bear

In April 2004, after the prompting of my dear friend and fellow prayer warrior, Lynette, part of our family's story of God's sufficient grace during our time of grief at the loss of our twin daughters (November 1996) and our newborn son in (July 1998) was published in the short story anthology, *Encounters With God* (Family Christian Stores).

A year prior to the creation of the book, my friend, Tracy Sponsler, suffered the loss of her baby, Kelly, who was stillborn in March of 2003. When Tracy lost her baby, I was searching for a memory book to give her as a gift so that she could have a keepsake to honor her baby's life. It soon became apparent, as I searched, that there was not a memory book available that seemed to truly comfort and give parents a place to record the dreams they had for their precious child.

When Tracy showed me what she received from the hospital to remember Kelly, I thought, we can do better than this. We owe it to grieving parents to do better. Parents who have lost their children lose a lifetime of dreams. They should have more than a little Polaroid. While hospitals have made great strides in recent years concerning creating a memory and respecting the needs of parents to have time with their babies, time to say hello and goodbye, and time to process the shock and grief of the loss, there is still a long way to go.

That is how the idea for the *Dreams of You Memory Book* was born. God began tugging at my heart, planting the seeds and ideas for a memory book that would give parents a place to record their dreams — the lifetime of dreams that they had for the baby they lost — a beautiful book that would show "a treasured life had been here". We put it together in a binder format so that parents could add and adapt the book to fit their own tastes. It should have a place to talk about the pregnancy, the dreams mommy and daddy shared as they waited, to record baby's footprints and handprints, a place to talk about the baptism/dedication, to journal memories, write letters to baby, to write about the funeral service, to keep a lock of hair and other cards and keepsakes. It should be durable and lasting, not just a flimsy paper book. It needed to be beautiful, like our babies. It would contain inspirational poems and scriptures and soft, dream-like artwork.

As the ideas formed in my mind, I began in a primitive way. Many tears and prayers came forth as I cut and pasted in scrapbook fashion, painstakingly gluing buttons and lace ...

searching for just the right pastel patterns. I would buy any binder that seemed like it may work and put baby block stickers that spelled the words Dreams of You on the front. To create a dream-like state, I glued vellum overlays. Hours would be spent writing, searching poems and sayings … designing, cutting, pasting, perusing the computer for artwork. My initial efforts were time - consuming and had a homemade feel. While admittedly primitive, I had an idea of what I wanted in my mind, but was unsure how to produce it outwardly. It was an idea in the birthing process.

Just a mama in her basement, I called hospitals to set up meetings with the nursing supervisors to show my idea and to offer the books to them. Shockingly, a few actually allowed me … a little mom from a little town … to come and show them my little home-made idea. Some were very interested. Others probably just tolerated my simple efforts. Some did not like the idea that the book was written from the Christian perspective, with the hope of heaven and comfort from the Bible. Sometimes I reflect with embarrassment over my lack of experience and my painstaking attempts to create the book from the ideas within. I want to go back and show the finished product that we have now.

Lima Memorial Hospital was the first to offer our Dreams of You Memory Books to their patients. We are so grateful for their willingness to help us offer comfort and hope to grieving families.

As the requests came for books, (and at the prodding of my friend and fellow board member, Becki, the wise business woman) it was evident that something must be done to simplify the process of making each book. I couldn't continue to cut and glue each one by hand. So back to work I went, sitting for hours in front of the computer to create pages in pastel colors that could be designed and printed completely on the computer. That way I could just print them out, punch the holes and put them together. I found a yellow binder and created a sticker for our front cover. The process of making several books still took quite a bit of time, but it was considerably faster than the other way!

While pondering the needs of grieving moms, we thought about adding resources to our baskets, like the book *Empty Arms* by Sherokee Ilse and *I'll Hold You in Heaven* by Jack Hayford. Remembering the pain of leaving the hospital with my own ache of empty arms, it seemed a teddy bear for the mother to hold might be another item to add. I was searching for the right bear (at the right price). Nothing seemed adequate.

My mother said she had an idea. Soon, she found a perfect teddy bear pattern and made an 18 inch bear out of pastel fleece. She called her bears Comfort Bears, as it was stated on the folksy hand-written tags attached with delicate ribbon tied around the soft fluffy bear's neck. She put a grandmother's love and prayers into every one, working on them until the month before she went home to heaven. She was diagnosed with cancer the fall of 2005. The journey our family stumbled through as she battled the evil disease that consumed her body could fill another book. Again, His grace was and is sufficient. I will miss her until the day we are united once more in Heaven's glory (where I am certain she enjoys tea parties with Faith and Grace and baseball games with Thomas even as I write!)

As she grew too ill to continue her work, we prayed for God to provide the bears to fill our orders. One day, while sitting on our lawn chairs, watching the children splash around during swimming lessons, Kaye Shively volunteered to help sew the bears. Kaye formed the Helping Hands Ministry at my church, Harvest Fellowship. This group of ladies performs many helpful services with their gift of sewing. We are grateful to them for enabling (my mother) Kathy's dream of offering her Comfort Bears to grieving moms to continue.

This process of "evolution" (the evolution of ideas sent from the Holy Spirit as God guided our thoughts!) took over three years. With the help from Lon and Marty and the staff of Shipman Advertising, we created our own cover for the *Dreams of You Memory Book,* which is now professionally printed by Shipman.

The inside has been completely redesigned. More hours were spent in front of my computer. More prayers, more tears, more flowing ideas. The book is now a mahogany brown leather color. The title is still stamped in baby block design. We added a bear, sketched by my son, Timothy, a replica of mom's Comfort Bear. On the bear's heart, there is a miniature version of our baby Faith's footprint. The pages are an antique cream-color. The clip art, which follows a soft old-fashioned dream-like teddy bear theme, is a deep antique brown. In addition to the memory book pages, we have included our family's story in an effort to offer the same comfort to others that we received from God in our time of need.

Sufficient Grace Ministries for Women received a 501 (c) 3 non-profit status in 2005 thanks to our dear lawyer and friend, John. Families are never asked to pay for our products or services. We are supported through donations from individuals, businesses, churches, hospitals, and funeral homes. We based our ministry on this verse:

Praise be to the God and Father of our Lord Jesus Christ, the Father of compassion and the God of all comfort, who comforts

us in all our troubles, so that we can comfort those in any trouble
with the comfort we ourselves have received.
– 2 Corinthians 1:3&4

God comforted and carried us through our sorrow and grief to hope and healing. And it is our desire to offer that same comfort and hope to others.

We began with the Dreams of You Memory Book and Comfort Bears. Then, I started meeting with hospitals. Soon, I was invited to speak and offer presentations at some of the hospitals. I shared our story and presented the materials we had developed for bereaved families with organizations in our area.

In February 2006, I was invited by my friend and the man who delivered our Thomas and our James, Dr. Marcotte, to serve as the Keynote Speaker for the Grand Rounds at Good Samaritan Hospital. It was such an honor and privilege for me. I spoke on three objectives: 1. Encourage an Understanding of Grief from a Bereaved Parent's Perspective. 2. Realize the Importance of Compassionate Care. 3. The Need for Parents to Form a Lasting, Tangible Memory of Time With Baby. Tim came with me on the trip to Cincinnati, and it was amazing. Since that time, I have been invited to speak at hospitals, churches, and women's events, sharing our message of hope and grace and our ministry outreach. I pray for more opportunities to share as the Lord leads.

A little over a year ago, God sent an amazing woman into my life. My sweet friend Dawn was a photographer for Now I Lay Me Down to Sleep (www.nowilaymedowntosleep.org). NILMDTS is an organization I so wish existed when we walked this journey with our Faith, Grace, and Thomas. They provide an invaluable service to families who lose a child. When parents face the loss, or impending loss of their baby, a professional photographer will come and take pictures of the baby and family, capturing those precious fleeting moments. Dawn contacted me, asking if I could provide her with bereavement materials for the families she serves. We talked about adding baby gowns and bracelets.

Well, our talk was no accident to God, because he guided us to a gifted seamstress with an amazing heart. She donated the materials and her time to create beautiful gowns for tiny baby boys and girls that the world may barely know, but whose footprints are etched on hearts of those that walk this earth. Families have been blessed beyond words by the amazing gift of having something beautiful to put their baby in for their photographs. Our team of seamstresses continues to make baby gowns out of donated wedding dresses.

A week before Dawn asked about making memorial bracelets for the pictures and to have as a keepsake, a lovely mom who has lost a child herself, Marlene Carpenter, handed me a gorgeous bracelet she had made using Swarovski crystals. I called her when Dawn made the request and asked Marlene if she would be willing to make bracelets for the moms and babies. She was willing and also donates supplies and time to create the beautiful bracelets we offer today. In addition to the jewelry Marlene fashions for our families, she crochets beautiful gowns and wraps for babies born at every gestational age. It means so much to families to be able to clothe their babies in something beautiful that fits their tiny bodies ... something made with love. Interesting how even when the tiniest need arises, God already puts a plan in place and sends a willing heart to fill it! Where He guides He always, faithfully provides.

Through our website (www.sufficientgraceministries.org), hundreds of families all over the United States, parts of Canada, South Korea, Scotland, Singapore, the United Kingdom, Ireland, Australia, and more have received our materials. We were blessed and amazed again several years ago when A Place to Remember agreed to place our Dreams of You Memory Books in their catalog and on their website.

In 2008, Dawn passed on a blog address that changed my life. Angie Smith's blog tells the story of their baby, Audrey Caroline, and her family's journey through grief and healing. I didn't know that this amazing community existed, this blog world. As a writer I felt like I had found my people. As a mother with babies in heaven and on this earth, I felt an understanding that I hadn't found anywhere else. I never attended a support group in the thick of our grief. So, I haven't spent a lot of time surrounded by other mothers who have walked this path. When I started my own blog (http://blog.sufficientgraceministries. org), I again wished that I would have had this opportunity and connection when we walked through our losses. I was amazed that these women were allowed to really share the lives of their babies - to grieve with hope, to honor them, to share them with the world.

I often felt like I couldn't fully share my children, that it would make others uncomfortable or cause them pain. But, in this blog land, we find support, prayers, and love. I have formed a bond of friendship with these women, who have walked where I once walked. Women who love the Lord and serve Him, women I have never met, but I'm honored to call friend. They have inspired me, encouraged me, and blessed me with their beautiful stories of our Father's amazing, all-sufficient grace. For so many years, I was silent, carrying this grief in my heart. When I found my voice, I could no longer be silent. And, the gift, the release, has meant sweet freedom to my soul.

We have other projects we are working on, as well. Tim and I desire to serve the Lord through the gift of music He has given us. Tim plays guitar, and I sing. We currently serve by playing at local churches, festivals, and other events. I also share our family's testimony and the sufficient grace we have experienced as the Lord carried us through the loss of our children, and continues to heal our broken places.

We have been blessed and amazed as we watch the body of Christ work together through this ministry. Our friends and fellow Christians have offered encouragement, prayers, donations, time, and abilities to support this ministry that God has given us. It is a humbling, beautiful thing to witness! We are so grateful for all that the Lord has done, and for the willing, generous hearts of His people.

Chapter Fifteen
Walking With You

He has sent me (Jesus) to bind up the brokenhearted …
To comfort all who mourn, and provide for those
who grieve in Zion-To bestow on them a crown of beauty instead
of ashes, the oil of gladness instead of mourning,
and a garment of praise instead of a spirit of despair.
– Isaiah 61:1b-3

Walking With You is part of the online bereavement support we offer to grieving parents. Below, you will find excerpts from our online support posts on the Sufficient Grace Blog. Others are free to share their journey and encourage one another as they come together from different places on this path of grief and hope. More information can be found on our website: www.sufficientgraceministries.org.

It is our prayer that all parents who walk this path would know that they do not walk alone. There is hope and comfort in the arms of the Lord.

The Night Walking With You Was Born
Tonight my sweet friend, Dawn Marshall from Marshall Photography met with my other dear friend, Toni (and me) to do a photo shoot for our upcoming support project. It had been a gray

drizzly day, raining lightly off and on. When the time came for our little shoot, it started to pour buckets of rain.

Of course it did. At first I thought, what is going on? What a disappointment that the rain would increase in strength as we met to take pictures. I heard thunder rumbling as we huddled under our umbrellas (which incidentally each had their own unique imperfections: mine had pokey things sticking out, Dawn's had a big hole in it, and Toni's was lopsided. And, yes ... I'm sure there are metaphors in that observation.), while I apologized profusely. The children of these two sweet mamas huddled together in their vehicles as the rain splattered down the sides and into the waiting mud puddles.

The rain poured. The thunder rumbled. And we walked in our cute shoes through the mud puddles into a dark alley that said Do Not Enter, while we huddled and shivered under our umbrella, gingerly navigating our steps to avoid more serious potholes. And, it struck me. The beauty of it. The realization that our God was still in control even as the rain poured. It was no accident that the skies darkened and the rains came down. The mud puddles, the foreboding alley that Dawn had suggested as our location. No accident. My original idea was two friends walking down a lovely tree and flower-laden path. How inappropriate that would have been. How unlike the message that we really meant to send. How not representative of walking together through the stormy paths ... through the dark sorrow of grief. Through the valleys. The point of what God has laid on our hearts is that we are willing to walk with you through those dark painful places ... and not so much that we are willing as that our God is willing. He is willing to walk with us ... and places that desire in our hearts to do the same.

And that walk, it's no flower-laden path. It is a dark alley with old jagged concrete, filled with mud puddles and Do Not Enter Signs. Dark and foreboding ... if we look with our human eyes. That walk is not for the faint of heart. It is the nitty gritty stuff of life and death, loss and hope, pain and healing, sorrow and joy. It is a bitter cup that one day becomes a soothing sweetness to your soul, but for a time breaks you into pieces. And, on that walk, it's unpredictable. The rain pours. The tears flow. The mud rises. That's what we see, at least.

Internally, the Lord is working. In the place we cannot see with our eyes, the heart is being shaped and mended, formed into a more beautiful instrument of love and grace than it was before we took that walk. Inside, our soul is being healed and filled up, even as the rains fall ... even as we feel poured out and empty. When all we see are ashes, He sees the beauty that will come from them. When we behold the darkness before us, surrounding us, smothering us ... He sees the light that He will shine in those dark places.

There are moments on that walk when we feel we cannot go on. Moments when a friend comes alongside us to point us again to the One who sustains us. A friend to lift us in prayer. A friend to allow us to lean on her as she leans on Him. A friend, who is not afraid to walk through the valley in the rain, with a storm mounting. She is not afraid, because the Lord is her strength and her shield. She is not afraid because she doesn't walk alone.

And because He has walked with her through the valleys and the storms, He has sent her to walk with you. And He will carry you both through the rain, through the storm, through the unknown dark alleys to secure, dry ground.

Whether you are a newly bereaved mother or a seasoned mom who has watched the Lord make beauty from ashes in her life. Whether you need someone to lean on or you are the shoulder that can bear the burden, we hope you will walk with us as we are walking with Him. We hope you will join us with our broken umbrellas, with all our little quirks and imperfections in our various stages on this walk, as His grace washes over us in the pouring rain.

Chapter Sixteen
Grieving as a Couple

More thoughts on the effects of grief on marriage from
WWY blog posts:

Tim and I were married very young and we had a two-year-old when we faced the loss of our twin daughters, Faith and Grace. I had endured a long and extremely difficult hospital stay that caused a great deal of stress and concern for my young husband. We were twenty-one years old at the time.

Losing Faith and Grace was such a shock for us. We had prayed and hoped for a miracle. And, honestly … I just didn't think that our babies would be among those that didn't make it. Maybe I was just young enough that I still thought I was invincible and that covered my children as well. I don't know what Tim thought at the time, and I was too absorbed in my own pain to ask. Just the same, we were shocked and devastated.

I wish I could remember clear details, but it's very fuzzy for me. I do remember Tim missing me and worrying about us during the long hospital stay with Faith and Grace. It took all my strength to survive, so I didn't feel the missing as much at the time. I remember how he tried to make me laugh. I remember his smile when we found out we would have identical twin girls, and the anguish on his face as the tears fell while he stood beside me as I held our baby girls and sang Amazing Grace. How he slept in the recovery room watching some random movie with me. I can still feel the ache of leaving the hospital with empty arms and a canyon of emptiness in my heart … and later, leaning on him for strength as we stood by their grave on that cold November day. And … the agony of sorrow when he went back to work. He held me often during those early days as I cried.

Even while we were in the hospital, I knew that we were forever changed by the loss of our girls … that we had shared something that only the two of us could ever really understand. It separated us from the rest of the world, and bound us more solidly as one flesh. I believe it drew us closer. He was quiet with his grief, having to remain strong. He needed to return to work right away to support our family and pay the mountain of medical bills.

Months later, we began trying to have another baby, and I think Tim wanted to help ease the ache of emptiness for me … for both of us. I have often felt a great burden for the dads who grieve for their babies in a world that doesn't allow them to express their feelings openly. They have to be strong. **A father doesn't just feel the weight of his own loss, but the pain he sees his wife enduring, a pain he can do nothing to fix. A pain he couldn't protect her from. He couldn't protect his family from this.**

Facing the choice, he was quiet, but seemed relieved when I chose to continue the pregnancy. He supported that decision. As I watched him agonize over the fact that he was helpless to protect our family from walking this path again, I struggled with the burden of being the one who brought this pain on our family. I know that wasn't really true. But, I felt that burden. And, to this day, one of the hardest things - the thought that brings tears to my eyes each time I think of it is the grief of Tim and Timothy - and the fact that I couldn't spare them of this pain. The sorrow it caused them to watch me carry our sweet Thomas, knowing we would have to say good-bye to him. I'm so grateful for the time we had with him, grateful we chose to trust God with his life. And, I know there was nothing I could have done to prevent the grief we all felt. I know that with my mind.

Tim was quiet and distant as the time grew near to meet our Thomas. The pain caused him to delve deep into a protective shell. I clung to the Lord for strength, and leaned on Ginny and Dinah, as he wrestled with what was happening within.

When Thomas was born, the pain was so great for Tim. I felt the joy of meeting Thomas, while Tim's sorrow broke forth heavily. We leaned on each other once more in those early days, and he respected that I needed to talk about and remember our children and I respected that he often needed me to do that with someone other than him. After the initial days of grief, we talked little about the experience to each other. This time when the desperate ache for a baby to fill my empty arms came, neither of us had the courage to say that we were ready to try for another baby. Fear of another loss was so strong. Tim was very protective of that.

When we were surprised with James's conception, it was a time of great trepidation and anticipation. I wanted to hold on to hope and joy … knowing that I would not get this chance again. I wanted to cherish every moment I was given with this precious baby. But, for Tim, all that we had endured had taken its toll, and the stress of watching me struggle through another pregnancy and the possibility of another loss was just too much. It was a very difficult time in our marriage.

There is so much about that time between us that needs to stay between us. But, I want to share a few things because I know that many of you struggle with the fact that men and women grieve differently. It's one of the main things we are asked about ... marriage concerns and grieving differently.

Every individual is unique in their grief. He may be quiet, distant, angry, protective, or tearful. You may feel like talking about your babies, need to be close, angry, tearful, or distant. You may not be feeling the same things at the same time. This can cause division and resentment when we do not understand that our spouse is still grieving, even if he or she is not grieving the same way we are.

Tim and I shared this sorrow ... and this entire journey, but we rarely talk about it. We are able more now than we did years ago. We have always respected each other's need to grieve differently and communicate that grief in different ways. It doesn't mean that we did not offer love and support to each other. We did and we do. But, sometimes, I went to a friend to talk or share a memory that I thought may be painful for him. And we didn't let that come between us. It's O.K. that he didn't want to go to a special remembrance service years later. And it's O.K. with him that I did need to go. I think it's important to recognize and free each other from expectations here. It will prevent being hurt when we feel that our expectations are not met. And, it prevents resentment and division from forming between the two of us.

We are not some perfect example to be held up for display. Indeed, our path to the beauty we experience today was once covered in tattered ashes of brokenness. It is a messy journey, and we often didn't "do it right." We are truly bathed in God's grace. I could write several statistics saying that there is no way Tim and I should still be married. We were married young, became parents at a very young age, came from divorced families (generations of divorced families actually), and we lost three of five of our children by the time we were twenty-three years old. Yet, here we are, loving each other and the God that kept us through it all. I don't say that as any great success on our part, but as a testimony to the greatness of the God we serve and the power of His grace that is always sufficient. We share a love today that is deeper and sweeter because of where we have walked. It is true that our God does "make all things beautiful in His time."

Here are just a few words of wisdom we have gleaned:

1. Respect each other's need to grieve differently. If at all possible, do not do things that may bring pain to your spouse. At the same time, do not deprive yourself of doing the things you feel you need to do to honor your baby your way. Find a way to honor your baby that also honors the feelings of your spouse.

2. Find time to laugh and do things that you enjoy together. Grieving is hard, heavy work. Find some time to keep it light.

3. Keep life as simple as you can. Try not to take on too much for your family schedule. Protect yourselves and each other from extra stress or things that may bring unneeded sorrow.

4. Find ways to honor the memory of your baby as a family.

5. Communicate with love and respect.

6. Take comfort in physical affection. Do not turn away from each other, but turn toward each other.

7. Pray together and for each other. God is able to mend your broken hearts and keep your marriage. Guard your marriage and bathe it in prayer. You may feel too weak to pray sometimes. That's O.K … .saying, "God, help me … it hurts too much to even pray." is still a prayer. It's been a prayer of mine many times.

Two are better than one,
Because they have a good reward for their labor.
For if they fall, one will lift up his companion.
But woe to him who is alone when he falls,
For he has no one to help him up.
Again, if two lie down together, they will keep warm;
But how can one be warm alone?
Though one may be overpowered by another,
two can withstand him.
And a threefold cord is not quickly broken.
– Ecclesiastes 4:8-12

Chapter Seventeen
Sibling Grief

Timothy was two years old when we were expecting Faith and Grace. His little life was turned upside down by my extreme illness and constant vomiting. Then there was a long hospital stay and little contact from me. Of course, he was doted on by his grandmas (my mom and Tim's) ... so much so that when I finally returned from the hospital, I had to peel him off my mom. He was getting used to the spoiling!

When Faith and Grace passed away, I told him as simply as I could, in language he could understand. He has always been a very perceptive person and a deep thinker. I told him that Faith and Grace were very sick and too sick to stay ... that God took them to heaven to heal them. I shared that He gave them new bodies in heaven ... bodies that were perfect and they would never be sick again. He seemed intrigued about the fact that they would have new eyes to see differently than we do.

In the weeks following their passing, Timothy drew pictures of his sisters (stick figures with really big heads!). He would sometimes give me a picture when he saw me crying ... to "make me feel better." He knew instinctively how much I missed them. I ran a home daycare at the time and during the early weeks of my grief, I was not working. For Timothy, that meant no children filling our house with life. Lonely and sad, sometimes he would stand at the window and say, in the saddest little voice ... "no kids coming today."

He loved to talk about his sisters and look at their pictures. He didn't seem to notice their brokenness. That was so refreshing to me, because I didn't see their brokenness either. As time went on, others grew uncomfortable or tired of hearing about Faith and Grace. But he never did.

We would talk about what heaven was like and what they would be doing in heaven. On their first (and subsequent birthdays), we would celebrate together (with my friend Ginny sometimes) with cookies and cupcakes ... pink, of course for our little girls. He would blow out the candle. We would talk about them playing in heaven and Timothy decided they would be wearing Barbie pajamas! I loved his child-like faith ... and I loved his openness in sharing about his sisters. Sometimes he would even run to get their picture when a visitor came ... making others uncomfortable. I loved his lack of inhibition. And, truth be told, I think we could learn from the way children experience grief. They live their lives and let out their feelings as they come.

With Thomas, Timothy had already experienced loss. So, he knew that pregnancy did not guarantee a baby. It broke my heart that he understood that harsh reality at the tender age of four. He prayed for this baby to stay. He prayed for a brother. A brother, he was given. But, we soon found out that this baby would not stay either. We told him that Thomas was very sick, and the doctors say he probably will not stay. He will go to heaven when he is born. It was so confusing, because Thomas was still alive in my growing belly.

He shook his head and his little voice sounded strangled as he choked out the words. "So, I won't get to hold this baby either. He will not come home." As I mentioned earlier, we reassured him with the hope of heaven and prayer. I hugged him. He was heart broken, but trying to be tough.

When Thomas was born, it seemed like such a whirlwind. As long as I walk this earth, I will regret not bringing Timothy to meet his brother when he was alive, not letting him hold him. Tim was in so much turmoil and I didn't want to add to it. I didn't know if it would be more painful or confusing to Timothy to meet his brother. But, that decision caused Timothy great sorrow … and I'm so sorry for it. Not meeting his brother and holding him was very hard for Timothy, and he talked about it for a long time. I did bring him privately to the funeral home, and he touched Thomas' cheek. But, his skin felt different than a baby usually feels. And the experience was not a comfort, but rather frightening for him.

We talked often about Thomas and what he would do in heaven also. We shared pictures. Timothy kept praying for a brother. We started traditions, like giving a shoebox filled with presents every Christmas to the Samaritan's Purse organization in memory of each child. In the early years, we bought Christmas ornaments to remember the babies. We had birthday celebrations, sometimes just Timothy and I, for many years. We would read *Mommy, Please Don't Cry* and *Someday Heaven.* We loved to talk about heaven. And those talks were a comfort to my heart as well as his.

In the fall of 2000, God answered Timothy's prayers and blessed us with another pregnancy. Timothy spent the time praying that this baby would stay. I would say that I hoped the baby would stay … and that I was praying, too. We almost lost James, and there were complications in the first and second trimester. I don't think I shared those with Timothy. His prayers for his brother to stay were so heart-wrenching. He was six years old by this time. So young to have faced such serious truths of life and death.

His brother, James, was born on May 3, 2001. And, this time, he came to the hospital. He finally held his brother, with a sigh of relief. James came home. And, he doted on him lovingly (for the first couple years, at least!).

When my mom passed away in October 2006, after a grueling battle with cancer, Timothy walked the path of grief once more - this time, as a young man. My mom was "his place" where he was always adored … loved … accepted, just as he is. She was his person, the one who loved him unconditionally and made life feel like it was going to be alright. He would talk to her when he didn't feel he could talk to me (And yes, I wish he never felt that way … but, sadly during his early adolescent years, he sometimes did.). His grief now is more like a man … and he didn't share it with me for a few years. Now that he is older, just recently graduating high school, he talks more about the loss of his grandmother and its impact on his life. I know that it was heart-breaking and life changing to say good-bye to her. And, I know all of the loss he has experienced has shaped his heart and his life. He had to learn very young what most of us don't know until we are much older. It has given him a seasoned wisdom beyond his years. He accepts the reality of death much differently than his peers who have had little experience with loss. It shapes the way he approaches life and gives him an eternal perspective most people his age are not capable of grasping.

Sometimes, we do still talk about what life would be like with all five children here in our little house and what they would be doing now. We have always focused on the hope of heaven, the truth that we will see our loved ones again someday. And there will be no more good-byes, no more tears. And bodies will not ever be sick or broken.

And I heard a loud voice from heaven saying,
"Behold the tabernacle of God is with men,
and He will dwell with them, and they shall be His people.
God Himself will be with them, and be their God.
And God will wipe away every tear from their eyes;
there shall be no more death, nor sorrow, nor crying.
There shall be no more pain, for the former things
have passed away."
Then He who sat on the throne said,
"Behold, I make all things new." And He said to me,
"Write, for these words are true and faithful."
– Revelation 21:3-4

I just want to encourage you to talk to your children. Include them as much as possible in the process. Share moments and make memories with them that include your babies in heaven. Realize that siblings are grieving as well. Be available to talk and listen. Answer their questions simply and age-appropriately. Shower them with love and reassurance. Keep their schedules stable and structured. Routine can be reassuring. Share comforting scripture about the promise of heaven. Pray with them and encourage them to pray. There are things, as I have shared, that I regret. It's difficult sometimes to make the best decisions in our own grief. Know that God's grace can cover our mistakes.

Chapter Eighteen
Supporting a Grieving Mother/Family

We spent a week on Walking With You sharing some of the things that people said to us while we were in the throes of grief, for better or for worse. Losing a child changes a person. This includes changes in our relationships with friends and relatives. In some ways, our new perspective reveals what's really important in life, and who really cares about us.

Every grieving mother I have met has been hurt by the words of someone else. Sometimes those words were well-intentioned from a person who was supposed to love the broken-hearted mother. Often words don't seem to have been thought out at all or may come from the heart of one who is bitter and hurting. Before I get too far into this, I just want to share a few thoughts in defense of those who have spoken words that caused harm, but did not intend to do so.

I have been a grieving mother, a mother who has walked this path more than once. A mother who has heard the hurtful words. A mother who had some friends who just couldn't be around me. Friends who didn't want to hear about my babies. Friends who didn't understand my loss. (I also have wonderful friends who did love me, pray for me, cry with me and come alongside me. They were few in number, but they exist. We have many friends who support our efforts to reach out to others, now. But the early days were lonely.)

And yet, I have also inadvertently said insensitive things to a mother who had several losses. Not knowing of her struggle to have children, and the heart ache of the losses she had endured, I said something about what a great dad her husband would be. She looked at me as if I had stabbed her in the heart. And, in fact, my words had done just that. Did I intend to harm her? No … absolutely not. But, I did, unknowingly. And, I of all people should realize that we never know what path someone has walked. We never know what they have endured, what they may be suffering. We should be careful with our words.

While talking with another mom who has lost a child a few weeks ago, she asked me what she should say to a mom who had just lost her young baby. She was delivering a Dreams of You Basket to her. She and I both knew the answer at the same time. There are no words. Just hug her. Maybe say you are sorry. Offer her your love and prayers. **But … the reason it is so hard to say the right thing … the reason so many people say the wrong thing … is because in reality, there are no words. There are no words that can comfort the ache … the canyon of sorrow experienced by a mother who has lost her child. None.**

My lovely friend Dawn made a great point a couple weeks ago in her comment on my *Where is the Love* post.

Dawn wrote:

"And when they raised their eyes from afar,
and did not recognize him, they lifted their voices and wept,
and each one tore his robe and sprinkled dust on his head
toward heaven. So they sat down with him on the ground
seven days and seven nights, and no one spoke a word to him,
for they saw that his grief was very great."
– Job 2:12-13

If only his comforters had continued what they started and simply stayed by Job's side, instead of trying to explain or give counsel. How many times we try to do things in love ... and in the end, we screw it up.

She and I shared a conversation about her comment. She talked about Job's friends ... and the fact that they just sat with Job in his grief for seven days. They wept with him. They just stayed beside him. They were willing to walk with him, but they said nothing. Now, we all know that Job's friends fell short after that. But, when did they get into trouble? When did they cease to be a comfort to Job? When they opened their mouths to speak in judgment of Job. Boy does that say a lot.

In the last several years, I have learned a great deal about grieving. I have watched many people walk through the sea of sorrow, and I've returned there myself a couple times. Today, I don't judge myself or others and the way we choose to walk this path. There is no magic timetable for grief or a right or wrong way to do it. And, when someone is walking this path, it is no time to judge their performance. They are just trying to survive it. Trying not to drown under the tumultuous waves that continually crash into us, over us, and all around us. It is a time for mercy and grace. Not judgment.

If you are someone reading this and wondering when your friend will get over the loss of her child, the answer is ... never. She will never stop missing her baby. In time, God can comfort her sorrow, ease her pain, restore her joy. But for as long as she walks this earth, she will have moments of missing her baby. She is forever changed. Don't rush her. Don't try to tell her she needs to move on. Don't assume that because she is grieving a certain way, that she is doing it wrong. Don't tell her how she should be doing it. She may feel sorrow. She may feel nothing. She may be angry. She may have peace. Or a combination of all of the above. Just let her and love her.

And, if you are a mommy in the new stages of grief, overwhelmed with sorrow ... wondering if you will feel this way forever ... please know this: You are forever changed. But, over time, those changes will become a beautiful part of the tapestry of your life. You will always miss your baby, but you will adjust to a *new normal*. You will not feel like you are drowning forever. You will laugh again and take joy in the pleasures of life again ... you will. Your life may be different, but it is not without hope.

I know it is intimidating. I know you don't know what to say in the face of such grief. Please know that we are grateful for those of you who do reach out, and don't be afraid to do it. We want to hear you acknowledge the lives of our precious children. We want to know that you care ... that you see our pain. We are blessed by your efforts and comforted by your love. We all need to give each other some grace in this area. And, please know that there were wonderful people who prayed for us, who sent heartfelt cards, flowers, gifts, hugs, and expressions of sympathy. We so appreciate and found great comfort in their efforts.

If I could confess something here, I struggle with knowing what to say or do often when a grieving mom comes my way. I have many times felt that my friend, Ginny, is much better at walking with a grieving heart than I. She has a gift for coming alongside someone who is hurting. I suppose that's what led her to be a nurse. I will always be grateful for the way that she laid down her own life to walk with me during the most intense days of my grief.

I have this ministry. But, I don't have all the answers. Again, it isn't about our abilities, but the Lord's ability to use us — to work through us, broken vessels that we are. We can't let our imperfections or the fear that we will not do it right, keep us from reaching out in love. There is grace, even for those of us who don't always say the right thing. I'm often much better at writing words than saying them in the moment. I like to take time to contemplate and edit myself. Unfortunately, life isn't always like that. In those moments, we can pray and maybe just say very little but be there for the grieving person.

We shared before that many of the most hurtful words came from someone who loved us. One thing to avoid is the clichés people often use when they aren't sure what to say. I personally have never been a fan of the phrase "God doesn't give us more than we can handle." There are a lot of things in life are more than I can handle. Burying my children is among them. It isn't about what I can handle, it's about the size of my God, and His ability to carry me through. His strength is made perfect in my weakness. I don't have to be strong.

Some have shared that they did not feel love at church - that they were met with judgment or ignored. Sometimes we mistakenly think that Christians aren't ever supposed to hurt or struggle. Grief doesn't fit well with that philosophy. It hurts and it tosses you about and turns your world upside down. Hurting doesn't mean that you lack faith. It just means that you have lost something or someone that you dearly loved. Even Jesus wept in the sight of the sorrow of His friends when they lost their brother Lazarus. I'm so sorry that we fail to love as we should, and I wish we would show the love of Jesus more in the body of Christ. My church as a whole has been wonderful, but I have been hurt by the insensitivity and ignorance of individuals. Perhaps unintentionally, but hurtful just the same.

Even bible verses can be twisted to cause pain in grief. Lynnette Kraft shares about this in her book, *In Faithfulness, He afflicted Me* in Chapter 3. Lynnette writes:

People quoted scripture to us verbally and in notes. These were also a great source of comfort, but on occasion, even a verse was the wrong thing. For instance, a verse like, "Count it all joy when you fall into various trials" would probably be better discovered by oneself than received from another. (Chapt. 3, pg. 55 *In Faithfulness, He Afflicted Me*)

Someone sent me a card with a verse about the seed that fell from the tree and died so that it could bear much fruit. Although, I understand what they were trying to say, at the time of raw grief those words stabbed my heart. I didn't want fruit, and I didn't want to think that my baby had to die so that there could be fruit. I wanted my baby! I didn't want to be judged on my performance, on how much faith I had or how well it was displayed as I carried this cross. That was a battle for me, one that the Lord's grace helped me overcome as He taught me a different way. But, many times the words of well-meaning friends were used for harm. I know that they didn't mean it, and they didn't understand. They hadn't walked this path. They could only relate with their own experience.

I have heard … "You can have other children. You're pregnant again! How many babies do you have now? Don't you wish you had a little girl? You really need to stop burdening your family with this grief. Now isn't the time for this. Get it together, Kelly. You just need to give this to the Lord. Christians shouldn't grieve without hope. Aren't you over this yet? It's really time to move on." And so many more.

Some of these words are true. We CAN give it to the Lord and Christians shouldn't grieve without hope. But, what does that look like? Does that mean we will never cry or hurt? Does it mean that we will never feel a moment of doubt or fear? No. We will feel all of those things. We will have bad days. The difference is that we know Who to run to. We know the One who is able to carry us through the dark valley. We take all the broken pieces of ourselves to the One who is able to put us back together again. And, when He does, we are no longer exactly as we were before. We are a new creation. And, what shines forth from the ashes is a thing of great beauty.

There is a freedom and a joy on the other side of grief that would have remained unknown to me under different circumstances. While I never would have asked for this path, I can see many beautiful gifts … and yes even fruit … from having walked it. There is a love my family would have never known. And, there are things I would not have experienced. But, in those moments of early grief, I probably wasn't ready to hear the promises of things to come. I just needed someone to weep with me, pray for me, and walk with me. Someone to get it.

As we emerge as that new person, we are different in many ways. Perspective changes. What once seemed so important no longer matters. It is replaced with things you never thought much about before, but now realize matter a great deal. While we will heal and joy will be restored in our lives, we are forever changed. Our very personality may even change. We will never get over losing our children. Not that we wallow in grief forever. Not that we will never be fully healed and complete. We will, but we will have a missing place in our hearts until we reach heaven's welcoming gates. A place where a much loved, dearly cherished, longed for and dreamed about life once lived. A life that lives on in heaven ... the place we long for with great homesickness, at times. Our children will forever be part of the tapestry of our lives. They are part of who we are. Please understand that. We can no more deny them than we could our children who walk this earth with us.

What a gift my blog family has been, and how I cherish the love shown here. Lynnette Kraft has said before, in the days of early grief, how she longed for someone to be able to tell her that she would get through this ... that she wouldn't feel that way forever. I so longed for that, as well, after the loss of my babies.

Lynnette Kraft writes (from her blog June, 2009):

Right after Anna died I desperately needed somebody who had lost a child to tell me I'd be okay. I was so sick with grief that I didn't feel I'd ever recover. I couldn't imagine ever being truly happy again without Anna ... it just didn't seem possible. That somebody never came. I did recover though. God was all I really needed. My joy did return. God did turn my mourning into dancing.

God is enough ... and He has been enough for me, too. But, He is so good in that He always gives us exceedingly and abundantly more than we can ask or imagine. He gives us each other to walk alongside one another on this path. Even though God has also turned my mourning into dancing, I so treasure the online community of mothers that walk together. And, because we have walked there, because He has traded our tears for songs of joy, we can tell you that this grief will not last forever. You will not always hurt this much. Your joy will return.

I still cherish the fact that I can share my Faith, Grace, and Thomas on my blog. And, we are received unlike most places in our lives. There is no uncomfortable pause when I write their names. Indeed, many others write them and know them as they do their own. Oh, how that blesses my heart. And, I will never tire of reading their names - of knowing they are spoken. For, I am a mother, as are you, whether your babies live on earth or in heaven. You are a mother, just the same. As I've said before, I never would have chosen this path ... and I'm so sorry that you are walking it, now. But, I'm so grateful for the beautiful privilege of walking it with you. And, I'm so grateful for being the mother of these precious children, of all my children ... and the beautiful gifts that each one has brought to my life.

It is often very difficult to know how to minister to the needs of a grieving mother who has lost her child. There are no magic words to take away the pain of such a loss, and many find it overwhelming just to look into the face of such suffering. Here are a few suggestions from a mother who has walked this path more than once, to sum up this chapter.

1. Don't allow the fear of saying or doing the wrong thing keep you from reaching out in love. There are no perfect words. A simple "I'm sorry" and a hug can go a long way.

2. Acknowledge the baby. Refer to the child by name. It is often a blessing to a grieving heart to hear her child's name spoken. Do not think that talking about him/her will bring the mother more pain. The memory of her baby is always on her mind. Sharing can be a comfort. Be willing to listen. She may need to tell her story over and over again.

3. Those who are grieving are not always able to ask for help. Instead of saying, "Let me know if you need anything," just do something for the mother and her family. Be available, but also be willing to give space when needed. Bring a meal. Offer to watch the other children for awhile. Come over and sit with her, offering a listening ear.

4. Realize that your friend has been forever changed by the loss of her baby. Don't expect her to be exactly the same. And please understand that grief has its own time table. Allow her the time she needs, and remain supportive. Everyone grieves differently. Don't judge her choices or her *performance*. She may not react the same way that you think you would.

5. Avoid clichés such as "You can have more children" or "This was God's will". Even words meant to comfort can actually sting a grieving heart like salt poured into an open wound.

Rejoice with those who rejoice, and weep with those who weep.
– Romans 12:15

Chapter Nineteen

Some commonly asked questions answered on the
Walking With You blog:

1. Will I feel like this forever? When will I feel normal again?

This is a question I think many of us have asked ourselves at some moment in this journey. There is a point when grief can feel so overwhelming. Suddenly life as we know it has ceased to exist. We are thrust into this foreign land, this tumultuous sea that we cannot control or predict. The unknown surrounds us washing away the security we once knew. We long for someone who has walked this path to come along and tell us that we will not feel like we are drowning forever. While we will never be exactly the same again, a new normal will settle upon us. Life will not always feel like this foreign land we have been flung into, without warning.

I used to wish that I had a fast forward button. The feeling was so unpleasant to me, that I just wanted to fast forward through the intense grief to the place of restoration. I wondered where the me I had once known had disappeared to and how I could get her back. Even in wondering, I knew she wasn't coming back, but I didn't know this new person.

Although I never when to a support group, and still maintain that I am not a support-group person (even though this is sort of like an online support group and I now host a local support group at SGM!), preferring instead to count on scripture, prayer, and close friends to walk with me in the valley, there was a point when I just needed someone who had walked there to tell me that I would not feel like this forever. That the smothering darkness of this sorrow would lift and light would shine again.

A few months in, I did call someone on a list I was given by the hospital. She reassured me that I would not feel this way forever. And, she was right. She also understood my feelings about the rest of the world moving on, while I was still grieving. She understood the way that you could only understand if you had walked this path. I guess that's why I started Walking With You … because I know that there is a point where we need to hear from someone who has experienced this that we will not feel this way forever. A new normal will occur, and we will be transformed, as well as completely restored. I am here to say that God has done that in my life through this journey. Take comfort in the hope of His promises for you.

You may want an exact answer … a time table. There isn't one. The truth is that there is no fast forward button. Grief is hard work, and it takes time. You cannot go around it. You must walk through it. You must allow the waves of the terrible sea to wash over you. They are cleansing … and necessary. And, the only way to keep from drowning completely is to cling to the One who is able to restore us. He does and He will make all things beautiful in His time.

2. I have heard this comment several times from grieving individuals. "I read your words, and I can see that there is hope … that God has restored your life. But … what I want to know is how? How do you do this? How do you get through it?"

I don't have a quick, easy answer for this. Everyone is so unique in their grief and their struggles. I clung to the Lord as if my life depended on it. And, it did. When I was too weak to hold on to Him, He held on to me. I read the bible, prayed, talked endlessly to friends who were willing to listen to me share the details over and over again. I cried buckets of tears. I was angry sometimes, felt forsaken and hopeless sometimes, wondered when this would end, and cried out for help to the Lord over and over again. It wasn't pretty. When we write words on a page, it all seems to be tied up so neatly in a package. It wasn't like that. I did not do this perfectly. I am absolutely not a poster child for the way to properly grieve. I don't think anyone could fill that role. We are all different, and we do the best we can. I wish there was a formula I could give you to get from the point of grief to restoration. I know the deep desire to get from that pit to restoration … from the ashes to the beauty. Boy, do I know. (Please keep in mind, it was 8 years from the time we lost our babies until I felt led to reach out and minister to others. I did not come to this place over night. God worked in my life over time … and He's still working on me!)

All I can say is to keep looking to the Lord, keep holding on to Him, keep believing His promises … even when your feelings don't match up. And know this: it's not about your performance. It's not about doing it right. His grace is poured out over you … and His grace is always sufficient. You don't have to find the way from point A to B … from ashes to restoration. Just trust the Lord, and let Him take you there.

In the mean time … just do the next thing, as Elizabeth Elliot says. Keep it simple. Take care of yourself. Put one foot in front of the other. Get out of bed. (Some days!) Brush your teeth. Don't look too far ahead. Just do the next thing … whatever it is.

3. How do we know when we should try to have another baby?

I have been asked this question several times by parents ... and even medical staff (seeking a parent's perspective). There are books on the subject that could cover the medical, physical, and even emotional aspects better than I ever could. And, my answer may seem almost like a cop-out. What I am going to tell you is to pray and trust the Lord with this. Go ahead and read about the other aspects. They do matter. But, God is in control of all of those things. And, He is the Giver of Life, the Great Physician, the Creator, and the One who knows the beginning from the end. Who else would we trust for something so big?

Now, there are practical things to consider. Your body needs time to heal, as does your heart. Consult your physician to determine physical readiness. Talk to your husband; this is a decision you should make together. And ... pray, pray, pray for the Lord's guidance.

Again, there is no formula for knowing when you are ready, and you will probably always have some anxiety about having another baby. I was once asked at a conference for medical staff how my husband and I determined we were ready to have another baby after losing three of our children. The answer was, "We didn't."

After Faith and Grace, we were desperate to have a baby to fill our empty arms. We tried as soon as we were able. There were physical complications that hindered us for about a year. When we conceived Thomas, we were excited and nervous, prayerful and anxious. After Thomas passed away, we did not leap into trying for another baby. Although I wanted to think it was possible someday, Tim wanted to protect our family from walking this painful path once more. Still very much wanting a baby, we did not want to walk through another difficult pregnancy that could end with the loss of another child. We never decided to try again. And, I don't know after that if we would have been able to make that decision on our own. While on birth control, it was decided for us, because James was conceived. The pregnancy was difficult physically and emotionally. We almost lost him early on. Tim and I struggled clumsily through by the grace of God. And miraculously, James was born and lives to tell the story. And, even more miraculously … our marriage lives to tell its story.

4. Don't forget about the dads.

Definitely not. Dads are often forgotten when parents are grieving. Maybe because they sometimes do not show their grief outwardly the same as mothers do. Many fathers seem less comfortable sometimes with the outward display of emotion. Maybe because people are even less sure how to minister to grieving fathers than grieving mothers. My heart goes out to dads in this situation. Often, I think of how they are not only grieving the loss of their child, but they are dealing with the added weight of not being able to ease the sorrow of their wives. Most men feel the need to protect and fix things. They couldn't protect their family from this tragedy, and they can't fix the brokenness of grief. That is extremely difficult for a husband and father. Add it to his own grief, and it's often unbearable. I am not a man, and do not feel qualified to give a man advice on this. But, I will say that it would probably be helpful to talk with other men who have lost children. And, keep on communicating with your wife. I have read many fathers write of their struggle with that, and encourage one another not to bottle it all up and pull away. Please know that we see your pain and we love you even if we don't know how to help. And, please keep seeking the Lord, and leaning on Him. He is big enough to carry you and your family … and, it's O.K. to let Him. Sufficient Grace now offers a beautiful resource booklet written from the hearts of fathers we've walked with over the years called Walking With You for Fathers.

5. Where is God in all this brokenness?

The question hangs in the air. It's the one I struggle to answer when face to face with such grief. The one that won't tolerate some well-thought out response with flowery prose. The one that looks skeptically at the scriptures that promise comfort and peace. It's the one I don't have an answer to … at least not a worthy answer.

Where is God in all this pain … and why did He let this happen?

Sure, I could wax poetic with a thousand clichés and pat answers. There are beautiful scriptures … examples of faith. Words that are true and right. But, when standing face to face with the raw agony of a heart twisted in that level of pain, sometimes I am rendered speechless. Sometimes there are no words, no answers.

I could say that this world is not the one He intended for us. The suffering, grief, and destruction are part of life in this fallen world. They are not Who He is. He is the love that carries us, the peace that sustains us, the grace that offers redemption. He is in the beauty born of the ashes.

My words will not fill the ache of a mother's empty arms or the agony of living life on this earth without the one she loves. Many times, I say nothing or very little and simply offer prayers and/or scripture. But, sometimes I long for something to say … some hope to cling to.

In April 2010, a blog friend K., wrote a post, wondering about God and His intentions ... wrestling honestly with her grief and the sometimes hurtful words of others. The response that poured out of me (along with buckets of tears) was the closest I have ever come to saying what I wish could be said to an aching heart. Still, the words are far from adequate. Below is a comment I left on her blog:

K.,

I am so sorry people have used words that are hurtful. I'm reading your words with tears pouring down my face, so sorry for the hurt you are feeling. I can feel the strength of it through your words. The anger ... the pain ... the feelings of abandonment. They are bigger than anything else right now. Right now, there are no perfect answers or words tied up in a neat bow to explain the suffering and death of your sweet baby girl ... and the continuation of loss you feel facing infertility. There are no words to make that better or explain why. I know the pain is bigger than anything else ... that you feel like He has let you down, turned His back on you. You are in the thick of grief ... heavy, relentless, merciless grief.

You may read my blog and see where I am now ... it isn't a place I've always been. The process of getting beauty from ashes is no walk in the park. There were years of healing, brokenness, restoration, surrender, and learning to trust Him. He is still piecing some things back together in my life.

The words I want to tell you are going to seem so cotton candy right now. But, they are true ... and maybe you can take some comfort in knowing that they are coming from someone who has walked through some stuff.

God doesn't intend suffering, pain, death, sickness, cancer, grief ... any of it. He never intended it. He isn't the author of it. And, as a loving Father who values you enough to send His own Son to suffer horribly and die in your place ... He takes no pleasure in your pain. He loves you and His heart breaks for you ... with you ... I get that you can't feel Him right now ... that the pain is too much. I get it, and so does He. When I even try to think of the depth of your pain, it seems like such bologna as I'm writing it ... knowing that you are not in a place to receive this right now, and desperately hoping that my words do nothing to pour salt in your gaping wounds ...

You may be thinking ... O.K ... He didn't intend it, but He allowed it. He didn't stop it. He didn't protect her. He didn't protect me. You're right ... He didn't stop it from happening ... and I don't have an answer for that. Not one that will make it better. His ways are not our ways ... and only He sees the beginning from the end. It is true that there are beautiful things that come from the ashes of our brokenness. And God can use all things in our lives to shape and mold us.

But, when you are in the pit sinking ... where you are, those words sometimes don't help ... and may even bring hurt. Who wants to hear about being shaped and molded when your arms are aching for your baby, your body is broken, and your heart is in pieces, and your mind is plagued with memories of the suffering of your precious child? You can't see the hope of that promise from the pit. Can't feel the comfort of it. That doesn't mean it isn't there ... doesn't mean that He isn't there ... and I know me saying it doesn't make you feel better.

From my pit ... I didn't want to hear about God's will ... didn't want to hear about the fruit that would come ... didn't want to count it all joy ... didn't want the witty words and well-meaning verses ... didn't want the pretty flowers ... certainly didn't want to listen to any miracle stories. Almost every promise from scripture or well-meaning words from Christians brought pain. I just wanted my babies. And I just wanted my mother. And … they weren't here …

For a time, I didn't want to hear about the promises and hope.

But … in time when, I did, I wanted to hold on to the promise of the joy set before me … wanted to know that although weeping may last for a night … joy would come in the morning. I didn't know when morning would come to my house and stay … but one day, on my knees, crying bitter tears … I felt myself surrender all that I had wanted and just let Him carry me. There's no formula or timetable to come to that place … and it sounds so easy and tied up in a pretty package as I'm writing it right now. It wasn't. And, it wasn't a place I could come to on my own …

Here's the thing, I believe as the bible says, the rain falls on the just and the unjust. Whether we are Christians or not, we will find suffering and trouble in this world. It's a guarantee. We will walk through these valleys with or without Him. The bottom line is … I'd rather walk through it with Him than without Him.

There is unspeakable beauty that has grown in our lives from the ashes of our sorrow. I don't believe that God sent the sorrow and loss … and I never would have chosen it. But, He has used it to make us who we are … to draw us to Him … to teach us to love one another. I'm saying that, not to rub salt in your wounds, but to tell you that there is hope for healing. Even in this darkness … light can shine again.

And, K … even when you can't feel Him, He is holding you. He will carry you … He is carrying you. When you are too weak to reach for Him, He still holds you. When you are too angry to hear Him … to go to Him … He waits for you. And … no matter how hurt, angry, deserted, lost, hopeless, broken … no matter how long it takes … He will wait for you. He will be there with open arms.

He loves you with a relentless love. A love that can take your anger, your sorrow, your questioning, your doubt, your pain ...

His only intention is to love, heal, save, and carry you ...

You, my dear, are not a failure ... and no one has the right to judge your "performance" in the pits of grief. No one.

I hope you don't mind my long comment ... and all of my words. Words that I know do nothing to "fix" the brokenness. Please know that they have all been written in love ... my heart is breaking with you ...

I pray nothing I've said added to your pain ...
Love and continued prayers,
Kelly

Chapter Twenty
Ways to Remember our Children

On another Walking With You post, we shared the ways we incorporate the memories of our children into our family life and the beautiful ways that the lives of our children impacted others.

Faith and Grace went home to heaven in November, so Christmas was not far behind. Many people sent us Christmas ornaments in memory of our girls. Over the years, we have added ornaments for each of our children. After Thomas' passing in July of 1998, ornaments were added for him, as well. They are scattered throughout the tree along with the ornaments that our boys make in school that remind us of the way they are growing as they walk this earth.

I mentioned before our tradition of filling the shoe boxes for Operation Christmas Child. We do one in memory of each child in heaven. So, our family sends two girl boxes and one boy box. It has always been a blessing to us to remember our children in this simple way. We enjoy shopping for little gifts that we would give them if they were with us, and we are grateful that those gifts will be given to children in need.

In the early years, we had birthday celebrations. My friend Ginny and her children even shared a few with us. Timothy always wondered when he was little if they could see us celebrating. Then we would talk about what they may be doing. He would talk about what he would give them if they were here.

For many years, we did not have pictures of our heavenly babies on the shelves. But, they are there now, blended among pictures of our children who are with us. Faith and Grace's tiny, delicate footprints and Thomas' angelic little face both sit on our shelf, along with memorabilia that remind us of their lives. For they ARE living … in heaven's glory.

The greatest gift we have received from the lives of our heavenly children has been to know the sufficiency of God's grace and His ability to make beauty from ashes in our lives. He comforted us in our desperate grief. And, it is the desire of our hearts to reach out to offer that same comfort to other grieving families. Thousands of lives have been touched through this ministry. People have been comforted in their grief. Souls in our family have been saved as people turned to Jesus for comfort. Restoration is a beautiful, amazing gift to behold … the restoration of lives, souls, marriages. Thousands have read and know the names of these precious little babies through our little blog and this ministry.

Every time we are able to give a family a Dreams of You Memory Book or a Comfort Bear, or just to pray for them and reassure them that we understand their pain … .our children are remembered. And we are humbled to know that God values and uses every precious life. You know the feeling you get when you watch your child hit a baseball and slide into home plate or ride his bike for the first time or just anything to spread his wings and soar? Seeing another person's life impacted by the lives of my Faith, Grace, and Thomas gives me that same feeling. It isn't the reason I serve in this ministry, but it is certainly a blessing that comes from it. God's purpose for their lives is evident to us. More is being revealed as time goes on, and that is a great gift.

Praise be to the God and Father of our Lord Jesus Christ, the Father of compassion and the God of all comfort, who comforts us in all our troubles so that we can comfort those in any trouble with the comfort that we ourselves have received from God.
– 2 Corinthians 1:3-4

My friend (and fellow SGM board member), Holly Haas, has demonstrated beautiful ways to honor the memory of her daughter, Carleigh MckKenna Haas, who was diagnosed with a fatal condition called anencephaly. Holly had a beautiful prayer shower during her pregnancy, in place of a typical baby shower. Friends and family brought baby bottles filled with coins to be donated to a local pregnancy center. (You could donate to the charity of your choice.) They gathered around and prayed over her and Carleigh. What a precious memory for all of them, and a wonderful way to cherish Carleigh's life. Holly also had a belly casting party. Friends helped to make a cast of her pregnant belly, which she later had painted by a talented artist, as a keepsake and work of art in memory of their baby girl.

Holly and her family took a vacation. It was a great time to soak in the time they were given with their baby girl and to enjoy one another as a family. Families have gone to baseball games and Disneyworld, or other special places, while waiting to meet their child.

Stacy, mom to Isaac, wrote beautiful letters to her son while carrying him in her womb. She knew her time with him was short, and wanted to pour a lifetime of love into her time with her son.

.

Chapter 21
More Thoughts on Saying Goodbye, Dinah, and My Mother

This life is filled with goodbyes. The longer we live on earth, the more we will experience the ache of loss, through the avenues of death, change, and walking away. When I started writing this book, in 2005, my mother was still living. My dear friend, Dinah, so instrumental in my growth as a Christian and in teaching me to be the kind of wife and mother my family needs, still walked this earth, and spouted her thoughts through my telephone as we cooked and cleaned in our kitchens.

My mother left this earth in October of 2006, after a grueling fourteen month battle with cancer. Dinah, my second mother and dear friend, went home to heaven in February of 2011. More gut-wrenching goodbyes. More standing by the cold graves. More missing. I wanted to share a few blog posts in honor of these brave, beautiful women who shaped and inspired my life. Women who walked courageously beside me, even in the darkest of valleys.

This is the eulogy I wrote, words from my heart, read at Dinah's funeral:

Dinah exemplified the definition of a Titus 2 woman with her own flair, wrapped in zebra print and polished toenails. When I was young and newly married, she taught me how to be a wife, with her sweet, snarky way of telling it like it is. With her straight-talking ways, she drilled into my young, selfish, raised-in-a-household-where-women-were-in-authority mind the importance of honoring my husband and caring for my home ... and training up Godly young men. She walked with me through the deaths of my twin daughters, Faith and Grace ... and later my son, Thomas. She sat beside us as Dan delivered our son's eulogy under the blue sky with big, fluffy white clouds while the sun shone on our grief-stricken faces. One of a handful of people whose eyes looked upon our Thomas, she saw and appreciated his beauty. Her house was always the best place to have parties ... the best food and fellowship. Her special gift has been making her home a haven for all who entered, a gift that now lives on in (her daughter), Christy. She made the best apple pie on God's green earth, a gift I hear she has passed on to (her daughter), Anna. She prayed fiercely for everyone in her life ... no doubt her prayers helped keep my marriage together through the toughest years. She loves and "gets" teenagers ... and they love her right back. When in good health, she visited and encouraged, and genuinely loved those in prison as she helped deliver the gospel to them. In our most recent conversations, Dinah and I spoke of the miracle that ... "The most beautiful gifts in this life emerge from some of the most difficult suffering. It's in the hard stuff that beauty is born."

Dinah is my second mom. And, like my first mom ... cancer has stolen much from her. She toughed it out ... much like she toughed out everything else this life has dealt her so far ... with a perfect blend of grit and grace, trusting the Lord every step of the way. I love her dearly.

I always loved the way her house was adorned with touches of her: paintings she made, fabric draped across windows, fabric she *chose for its color and texture. Fabric she sewed with her hands. As I walked through her house during the past few days, I looked at her pictures telling the tale of a life well-lived and a woman well-loved, who loved well. I looked at the scripture scrawled across her beloved chalkboard and my eyes wandered to the kitchen table where we shared our revelations, our tears, our prayers, and most of all our unbridled laughter. I ran my hand across the table with the wild horses painted on it … the table she made with her hands, admiring the beauty of her work.*

I remembered our conversation after my mom passed. I was struck by how much the touches of a woman and her personality make up a home … how valuable a mother is to the life of her family. Dinah had talked then of her own mom's passing in those days when my wounds were still fresh, as I cried with the ache of a daughter who had no idea such missing could exist. She knew about the missing. She missed her own mother still … her mother Ruth, the one who always had painted finger nails and called me, "the girl who laughs". I can't help but smile as I think of the two of them in heaven having a big time, looking sassy and cute as ever.

In the waning moments of her life, I wondered for a moment, "What is the point of all of this?"
The answer lies in the look in her husband's eyes when someone shares how his beloved has touched their lives with her amazing faith. The answer lies in her beautiful blond daughters who love Jesus and are filled with the grace and grit she leaves behind. The answer lies in the legacy of photographs, pristine English riding competitions, girls on horses jumping fences, and her dog Sky's blue eyes that she loved so much. The answer lies in the face of her precious grandson, Eli who brought abounding joy to her heart.

It lies in the beauty of my marriage restored and flourishing, and countless others she prayed for … healed and restored. I think of all the night watches she lay awake praying prayers on my behalf … on behalf of my kids, my mother, my husband, her family, her friends, the prisoners she ministered to … .everyone she loved. The answer lies in those who proclaim the name of Jesus because she prayed and boldly shared the truth with them.

As I walked through her house trying to soak in pieces of her, I read some of her favorite quotes hanging in the kitchen. One was a reminder never to get too hungry, tired, lonely, or angry. Advice she gave me early on in my marriage, along with a myriad of other things. Another was "Most people die with the music still inside of them." I smiled, looking around at her eclectic, colorful house that so reflected her eclectic, colorful, snarky sweet personality. Most people might die with the music still inside them, but not Dinah. She held nothing back … not her opinions, her wisdom, her passionate love for Jesus and His word, and most of all her love for everyone around her. The symphony of her life was poured into the lives around her. Her symphony plays on in the lives of everyone who loved her. And, as the music of her life continues in ours, we also rejoice as we think of the celebration in heaven as they welcome home one of their own. Dinah always did love a good a party!

From the Sufficient Grace Blog: Tasting Heaven While Dressed in Funeral Clothes (March 1, 2011)

I laid out my dress, chosen with her in mind, searched through my drawers to find the elusive pair of black hose without a run, fastened the silver beaded necklace, slipped on the bracelet Marlene made for me, and smoothed the make up over my tear stained face. He pulled his suit from the closet and hung it on the door as we readied ourselves.

Funeral clothes.

Everyone who loved her was laying them out at the same time in their various homes, getting ready to say goodbye. Tears mixing with water droplets falling from the shower head. A ritual that becomes more familiar with the passing of time.

Laying out the funeral clothes.

The scent of yellow roses wafted throughout the sanctuary and draped her casket. I nodded in the direction of her zebra print top and stepped onto the stage for the sound check. She always inspired me to rise to the occasion and do the next thing. "Lord, help me be able to do that now ... help us." After adjusting his guitar strap, I sang a couple verses, breathing in the flowers and letting the song carry us. His peace was there.

The whisper ... "Just cling to Me ... I will carry you ... I will meet you there."

I nodded, knowing He would.

The joy of her heart, three years old with the blondest hair I've ever seen and the bluest eyes, stole my heart in one second as he clutched his big Floppy pony. He danced to show what Grandma Dinah was doing in heaven, and making tear stained faces smile. He stood by his Grandpa and folded his hands as he leaned into his mama. Pieces of her living on in him ... in all of us.

We bowed our heads, we took the stage, and sang our songs. (Tim played guitar, while I sang. One of her requests.) I thought of how she always inspired me to rise to the occasion. Even though I was being carried, I was grateful that He met me there so that I could honor her. We listened to the memories of her, and I clung to him. There's nothing more beautiful than the testimony of the life of one who loved the Lord and served Him with all of her heart. Precious. Precious in the eyes of the Lord is the death of His servants. Precious. Because death here means new life there.

Heels clicking on pavement and a sea of black suits made the procession. Driving through puddles in our funeral clothes, snow melting into mud. Heels sinking into the soft earth and gentlemen hands helping ladies over the puddles. Black suits huddled beside the grave adorned in our funeral clothes, breathing in yellow roses under a tent, February winds swirling around. Quiet weeping and scripture reading, heads bowed in prayer, hearts honoring a woman dearly loved. Her blond legacy beautiful, sitting in a row ... saying goodbye, beginning the missing. Full of the grace and beauty she leaves behind.

She knows how I feel about the grave and visiting the cemetery. She knows I'd rather focus on heaven, and she always agreed. Still, we stopped to lay one of her yellow roses on their grave, just a couple spots over, clinging to one another as if it were yesterday that we stood in this spot saying different goodbyes with the much younger looking tear stained faces. We walked away from the graves, heels sinking in the mud.

I'm always saying the only thing you can take with you to heaven is other people. If in heaven our riches are based on how many we take with us by showing the love of Jesus during our time on this earth, then our Dinah is a very rich woman. She touched so many lives in such a profound way ...

A funny thing happened … an amazing, miraculous thing. Dinah loved everyone in her life with all that was in her and she talked about each of us to the others. She described the people she loved in such detail that when we met face to face today in the place we came to honor one we love in our funeral clothes, we felt as if we knew each other. In heaven, scripture tells us that "we will know one another as we are known." I tasted that today.

Let me preface this by saying that I have an absolutely terrible memory. I am always forgetting names and everything else. But, today, many times I would see someone Dinah loved … a person I had never met or seen before, but I knew their names. I would say "Are you so-and-so?" And, each was the person that Dinah had told me all about. Each one knew me right back. It was as if we all knew each other and were connected by her love. That must be a taste of what heaven is like … knowing one another … connected by His love. It was a special gift. And, truly a beautiful celebration. Except for all the black and the tears, she would have loved it. She would been thrilled to see all the people she loved gathered together and knowing one another as we are known … no doubt she did.

One of Dinah's few requests was to be buried near my babies. And, so she was.

March 11, 2011:
Have you ever considered the word "cling" in The Old Rugged Cross? *I never had until the day we stood side by side, singing at Dinah's funeral. Tim's guitar music gently guided, and I sang the words. And, when I reached the chorus, my voice quivered for a moment as I sang,*

So I'll cherish the old rugged cross,
Till my trophies at last I lay down;
I will cling to the old rugged cross,
And exchange it some day for a crown.

"I will cling to the old rugged cross … and exchange it some day for a crown."

A crown which I will lay at His feet. I remember when Dinah and I talked about how He will turn our struggles, and our clinging to Him into crowns one day. Crowns we can lay at His feet in an act of worship. She had just gone Home, and I stood in her church, singing about the crowns and the clinging. And … He met me there.

You know, He always meets us there. Where ever He asks us to go, He is faithful to meet us there.

And, He's here, right now … in the laying down of my trophies, in the learning to cling to the cross ever closer.

In all of it, He is there.

March 7, 2011:
Last week was hard.

Going back to life and work so quickly after saying goodbye to Dinah seemed so surreal.

The weight of that reality for her family … heavy on our hearts, heavy on theirs …

A lot of heavy.

Tears fresh in my eyes as I walked into work, heavy with thoughts of her and images of grief-stricken faces parading through my mind.

Tuesday, Wednesday ...

By Thursday, I awoke once more with the heavy. The heavy of cancer's fury, of another goodbye, of all the sorrow this world offers, the reality of death, the missing of my friend. I looked in the mirror at the dark circles, the pale face, the worn look of one who has lived a lot of life in thirty-five years. I sighed heavily.

Another day, really?

Then, her words ... playing in my mind as they had so many times before.

"Cowboy up, Chicken Little. Just do the next thing."

She always called me Chicken Little. I have no idea why. She called her daughter, Christy, the same thing. A compliment indeed, since Christy is one of the most cool, beautiful, classy chics I know. She has a lot of her mother in her. Dinah liked the saying "cowboy up" ... meaning, "man up," "pull yourself up by your bootstraps." Dinah was a horse lover. I'm smiling now, picturing the cowboy boots under her casket. So Dinah.

"Just do the next thing" was a phrase spoken by Elizabeth Elliot ... a phrase we share here, often when talking about grief. When life overwhelms us, when things hurt too much ... just do the next

thing. It might be: get out of bed, brush your teeth, get dressed, go to work. Keep it simple. Give yourself grace. Dinah loved it and said it often.

So, I cowboyed up … got ready for work, got into the car, put one foot in front of the other … did the next thing. And, the next, and the next.

My Mother, September 18, 2009:

I can feel the September winds blowing in, filled with intoxicating memories that swirl around me, pulling me to that place of remembering moments I ache to experience once more and moments I never want to revisit.

Her birthday was in September. She turned fifty in a hospital bed, smiling as she ate a piece of my famous peanut butter cream pie … laughing carelessly with Pastor James (who incidentally, if I recall is among the two people in the whole world that did not profess my pie as the most wonderful thing in all the land!!). I was wishing she didn't have to endure the treatments much longer. She was determined to continue fighting.

I remember the day they said the word cancer. Actually, the oncologist spouted off a thousand other unrecognizable words. The kind of words that doctors use when they don't really want to tell you the findings. Words are easy to hide behind.

So, I finally said, "Are you saying she does not have cancer?"

"No," he said. "I am saying she most certainly does have cancer."

We walked out of the room, after she promptly told him that she would make him famous when she beat this cancer. He pulled me aside and said, "I need you to understand. It's not good. What we're dealing with ... It's very serious ... it's bad."

I guess it was easier to tell me than to look into her determined, beautiful eyes and say those horrible words. I appreciated his honesty, though. From the places I've walked, I'd rather know what I'm dealing with head-on. Once you know that you are not invincible ... once you know that it's possible to lose someone you love ... it's kind of always with you. That possibility.

I acted strong, nodding to the doctor, smiling at my mother. I felt the room start to spin, as I struggled to steady myself. I thought, "If I could just get to the bathroom before anyone notices." I barely made it inside the door, when I collapsed against the wall, my body shaking with the sobs of a helpless little girl ... not the strong woman of faith who had been carried more than once through the sea of grief by her loving Savior. But, a little girl ... whose mother was filled with a hideous disease that would steal her health, her body, her mind, and her life ... but couldn't kill her spirit. The sea of grief swirled around me, taking me captive with swells of images from other times when death's darkness stood mocking me ... as he threatened to steal the ones I love. I resisted crying "NO" from the depths of my soul as the memories washed over me, "I'm sorry there are no heartbeats ... they're gone" ... "a condition known as Potter's Syndrome" ... "incompatible with life" ... and, now ... "cancer ... it's not good ... very bad." I cried out to God, begging him to spare her ... to spare all of us. The sorrow had its way with me in that oncology office bathroom. Then I wiped my tears and walked out, stunned to face a life that held that ugly word.

She had "cancer of unknown origin" that they think possibly started in her lungs. It had spread to her lymph nodes, her brain, her bones ... it was everywhere! They said she had two weeks to six months. Two weeks? I couldn't even process that.

Thirteen months and tons of chemo and radiation treatments later, she sat in that hospital bed on her fiftieth birthday, lighting the room with her smile.

Growing up, we had a tumultuous relationship. I was so head strong ... always wanting to establish my independence. I spent most of her life missing all of her gifts and her beauty ... all of the things about her that made almost everyone who knew her fall in love with her. She had that kind of gift about her. She was so beautiful that people were held captive by her, even after the cancer treatments left her bald and thin as a rail. Didn't matter. She glowed with beauty. I spent most of her life missing it ... but when that word was spoken, everything between us disappeared. All I could see when I looked at her was the person God created her to be. All of the barriers between us tumbled helplessly when that word was spoken, and we could hug and laugh and share our hearts. As often happens, there were precious gifts, even in the face of such hideousness.

A few weeks after her birthday, we made the trip we had taken so many times down river road ... the one with all the big beautiful, extravagant houses. She had one picked out on that road. Only, hers was a little cottage with some hanging baskets on the porch. She always did prefer the simple things in life.

The leaves were a myriad of colors, exploding with the majesty of fall as we drove the winding path to the hospital for a visit to the ER to help manage her pain. It was just a "routine" pain management visit. We should have gone home later that day. We made jokes in the ER and giggled. I looked over and she was out cold, resting from the medicine they had given her. I felt the relief a mother feels when her baby is resting, knowing that she was not in pain at that moment.

They decided to keep her in the hospital over night. But it soon became clear that this time was not like all the others. She wasn't making sense and could barely wake up. When she did, she seemed like a little girl. I realized that I couldn't leave her in the hospital when I saw the condition she was in the next morning. She stayed for three days, and our very large family surrounded us as we tried to make sense of what was happening to our mother. In and out of consciousness, barely coherent. Where had she gone? I was just talking to her hours before. I can't describe to you what transpired next. The memories overwhelm me.

All of her doctors agreed that the next step was to take her to the Hospice Center or a nursing home. The cancer had spread throughout her body and it was only a matter of time. They said, "Maybe 48 hours." We had promised her that we would not put her in a nursing home, so we reluctantly chose the Hospice Center, thinking that it would probably only be a few days. We decided right away that we wouldn't leave her alone. So, we stayed there with her … sometimes all together, sometimes taking shifts. The Hospice people were amazing … and we are so grateful for their compassionate care.

Forty-eight hours turned into four weeks. For four agonizing weeks, she suffered in a way I never knew it was possible for a human being to suffer. We didn't sleep, except for a couple hours here and there when we would collapse out of exhaustion and then we would awaken in a panic. I sang to her, prayed over her, read scriptures. What I haven't described is the depth of suffering she endured. And I won't … I can't.

Only the ones who were there can understand what it was like. All I can say, is that it shook me to the core, trembling the very foundation of my faith. There were, of course, glimpses of joy in the midst of sorrow and gifts, even in the pain. She would awaken sometimes and we hung on every word, when she was able to speak. We never wanted to leave, desperate to soak in every moment we were given with her ... and wanting to be there, when she was finally carried Home.

I won't lie ... I begged God to take her Home. The suffering was so much, and I couldn't bear to see her in such agony. But the moment she left us, I realized that her leaving left us without her. And, the missing came. The missing was like nothing I ever thought possible, either. And, if anything, it has intensified with time.

Every September – October, when the leaves change and start to fall, and the autumn winds blow ... the missing washes over me anew ... and the memories flood my mind. I even resist sometimes ... wanting to just keep my eyes on Jesus and rest in His comfort ... wanting to just enjoy the land of the living. But, almost involuntarily, my body reacts. I can't sleep in September and my heart aches with the missing of her so deeply, I am overcome. The memories flood my mind. The sights and smells and feelings of fall all bring with it that time.

I walked into her house this afternoon to let out her dog (which we do for my stepfather every afternoon), and the ache was stronger that I could contain. I felt suddenly so desperate to see her sitting on her couch. It's been three years, and I don't know when I'll be able to walk into her house and not feel disappointed that she isn't laying on her couch. I walked through the house, stopping in the kitchen as I remembered the feeling of "home" when we would stand there, laughing about when we were kids and the silly things we did. We would tell stories in the kitchen. I washed countless dishes in that kitchen (those who have known me a long time always laugh, because it seems I'm always doing the dishes ... and have been since they've known me!) I thought about how if she were here, she would laugh at my "teaching Timothy to drive" stories and annoy me as she told him the stories of teaching me to drive when I was 16! I can't explain to you the bittersweetness of those memories or the depth of the ache. I can't explain how it feels to stand in the kitchen of your childhood home and feel like your "home" is no longer. It disappeared with her. But, if you have felt that kind of missing ... if you have lost someone you love like that ... someone who was your constant ... your definition of family, you know.

There are so many things that a mother fills in our lives. Sometimes I wonder where she begins and I end. So much of our mothers are part of the person we become. You know, you can't really brag about your kids to anyone but your mother. No one else gets it, cares, or loves them like she does ... like you do. She would love to hear about all the happenings in the lives of her grandsons. She would relish it and wallow in it like Grandma's do.

For the rest of the time I walk this earth, something ... someone will be missing. Several someones. Eventually that is true for all of us, and I know that. We will all lose someone we love. I also know that there is comfort in the arms of our heavenly Father ... that one day, we will see them again. One day, I'll laugh with my mother and hold my babies. I know, until that day, His grace is sufficient and He will carry me ... I know all of that. But, right now ... I'm just aching with missing ... swept into the memories of a September wind.

October 26, 2008:

I have her tea sets scattered throughout my house, and some are packed away, just in case I ever have the tea party we always talked about. I still want to pick up the phone and call her. I miss her laugh and her smile. I miss the way she fiercely loved her grandkids. She was their safe place ... where they were never judged and always loved. I miss putting the ornaments on the tree with her ... shopping at Christmas time. I miss her creative ideas and her enthusiasm for making things with her hands, and her heart.

She would love the way her Comfort Bears have gone all over the country (all over the world!) to fill the empty arms of grieving mothers. She would love the team of ladies who work to keep making her Comfort Bears with a grandmother's love and prayers. She would love to hear "Freshman Tim Gerken on the golf course with the low round of the day ... " on the radio. She would love to hear about his homecoming dance and reminisce with me about mine. She would love to watch James making a goal at soccer and listen to him trash talk his brother. Maybe she does see and hear those things from Heaven. Maybe she's smiling right now as she rocks her grandbabies. Maybe Faith, Grace, and Thomas are smiling with her as they watch our family. I'm so grateful she is there with Jesus and my babies, and not struggling here with cancer. No pain, no sorrow, and no good-byes for her. But still ... I miss her so.

Chapter 22
The Gathering of Women

Years ago, women gathered in kitchens and in neighborhoods. There was time to talk and sort through the stuff of life. There was a gift in walking through the changing seasons, sharing joys and trials alongside one another. There is often little time for the gathering now, as women are working outside of the home, and family schedules are full. As we send Dreams of You items around the world through Sufficient Grace Ministries, the gathering of women to sew and work alongside one another, has become a ministry of its own.

The teams of women gathering to sew Comfort Bears, wraps, gowns, make bracelets, and minister to grieving families share our stories and cry and laugh together. I've been held up by these beautiful women after being at a hospital all night with a grieving family, while serving as a birth and bereavement doula, collapsing from exhaustion and grief. The true beauty of that picture is the story hidden in that sentence. For the women holding me up, one a widow with three sons, who lost the love of her life and misses him with every fiber of her being every single day and the other … a mother who has buried three of her four children. An infant daughter, and a daughter and son in their twenties. The women holding me up, carry with them their own heavy, knee-buckling grief. And, yet, together we are strong enough to stand. We may walk with a limp, but we still walk with grace and beauty, the kind that comes from being carried. There are many stories, and many who walk with a limp at Sufficient Grace. There's something about a broken heart that seems the most willing to offer love.

Many who serve at SGM are broken vessels. God loves a beautiful, broken mess. He chooses the broken vessel, and delights in the beauty of it. As she lays there, feeling broken and helpless, her pieces scattered about, He steps forward, walking past all the expensive precious vases on the shelf, those pristine and without blemish, and He picks up the broken one. The one scarred and dented, abused and tossed aside by the storms of life.

He says, "I choose her."

I think sometimes he treasures the broken vessel because more of Him gets poured out through the cracks. The picture of His grace and love oozing through my broken mess, gives new meaning to this place of my not enough. For in my not enough, He answers … plenty. In my weakness, He makes strength.

Today, more than 500 families per year receive materials and support from SGM. That number is growing weekly. Approximately 50 people gather to serve in various ways, offering our broken pieces as God shapes them into something beautiful.

Among those who serve in the newest addition to the services offered by Sufficient Grace Ministries: the SGM Perinatal Support Staff and Remembrance Photographers. I and several other SGM staff members have been trained through www.stillbirthday.com to be certified SBD Birth and

Bereavement Doulas. Because every life matters, we are there to provide support for families facing a fatal diagnosis during pregnancy or a loss at any stage of pregnancy or after birth.

The first time Holly and I entered into this sacred ground to walk with another family was such a tender and precious experience for us. I know neither of us will forget the sweet baby girl we had the pleasure to hold and the family we had the privilege to walk with as they made precious memories with their daughter and granddaughter.

I wrote about our time walking on that holy ground on the Sufficient Grace blog:

Yesterday, I stood again in the place where heaven and earth meet.

It has been fourteen years since I felt Him brush past me, filling the room with soothing peace that knows no reason, and love that floods with warmth and hope, as I sang to my baby boy when he went straight from my arms to the arms of Jesus.

"Guess what I got to do," I said breathlessly, that day 14 years ago, when I called Dinah and Ginny, after holding my Thomas.

There is nothing so sacred this side of heaven. Nothing so precious. As the gift of life.

And nothing more miraculous and astounding than when heaven and earth meet for a moment. Anything is possible. Everything you hope for is real.

Grief and joy dance with abandon.

Because life … no matter how brief … is meant to be celebrated. Soaked in. Honored. Treasured. Because every life matters.

Holly and I had the incredible privilege of walking with

a family, waiting to say hello and goodbye to their sweet baby girl. We spent most of the night and the better part of the following day, standing on sacred ground with them. It was the first time we were able to offer in person support in those crucial moments … together.

As I scurried to pack my bag to take to the family, I ran through the SGM office, choosing crocheted gowns by Marlene, and satin wraps with pink lining and daisies made by Peggy, a Comfort Bear that several hands sewed and stuffed. Others glued hearts, others cut fabric. So many involved in the making of each bear. So many loving hearts and willing hands, working hours every month, so that babies that the world may never know will have something beautiful. And the families who miss them, will find some small comfort. I put pink bracelets made by Marlene into the bag. And, the *Dreams of You Memory Book* I wrote from my heart.

I wondered on the drive there what it will be like on the other side. I've been the mom. But, what will it be like to walk beside a family. Will they mind our presence? Will we be helpful? Will they feel as if we're invading this sacred place?

We have had the training. Read the books. But, what will the moment be like?

It was like breathing.

I remembered our SBD Birth and Bereavement training, and how important it is to focus on meeting the baby. Soaking in this time with her. Filling her brief life with memories. I remembered my own questions years ago, as I tried to answer theirs. And, I have never been so grateful that I was chosen to be the mother of Faith, Grace, and Thomas. Because they lived, I have something … however small … to give. Reassurance. Hope. From a mother who has walked there.

When we meet Jesus, the crowns we get for the way we serve him on this Earth ... the rewards. They aren't for us. They are so that when we see Him, and we are so desperate to have something to give ... to show our love ... our worship ... our gratefulness ... that we will have an offering. Something to cast at His feet, because He gave us so much.

And, when we look into the eyes of a mother about to say goodbye to her baby, there is nothing so desperate as the longing to have something to give.

When we met their sweet baby girl the next day, I felt such unspeakable awe of the gift that I could be allowed to behold the beauty of this precious little one. She was already wearing the wrap with the daisies that we brought for her. And, the bracelet was dangling from her mama's arm. As I slipped the bracelet on the arm of their daughter, I felt a stirring deep in my heart. The sacredness ... the privilege ... the nearness of heaven whispering. It was like putting the bracelet on my own little girls. Peace filling, surrounding. Oh, I remember this place well. This is the place where He is so near that you can reach out and touch the hem of His garment. I looked down in disbelief that it was my hands He would allow to do this most meaningful task.

I didn't get to put beautiful bracelets on the arms of my girls or an outfit on my Thomas. But, in that moment, it was if they were there too. And He whispered to my heart, "It will be this way for each baby you meet." I didn't do this for them. But, I can offer the opportunity for as many moms as I am allowed the privilege to meet. Because they lived.

I held her in my arms. So grateful for the beauty and gift of this little girl's life and the family that loves her dearly.

And, as we left, I felt the urge to call my Dinah and say, "Guess what I got to do."

I've struggled a little, at times, with this new identity. Being the person people think of when a baby dies. But, yesterday, I embraced the gift.

We get to go to the place where heaven and earth meet. We get to witness miracles. We get to be there to honor lives that few will see. We get to stand on holy ground. We get to offer beauty and hope in the midst of a pain.

And, because of the amazing hands and willing hearts of the women who gather to use their gifts to make beautiful items for tiny babies and their families …

We have something to give.

And … I am overcome. With the amazing grace of it all.

Chapter 23
Giving Thanks in all Circumstances

In the following WWY post, we challenged ourselves to give thanks for the gifts we received through the path of loss, hope, and healing and through the lives of our children. There is great healing and power in the simple act of giving thanks.

In recent years, I have been inspired by my online friend, Ann Voskamp, author of *One Thousand Gifts,* to take the time to count the gifts and blessings in each moment of this life. She would call the counting of the following gifts from such a sacred place of letting go and surrender, the "hard eucharisteo." Yes. But, the most difficult places of surrender also hold the sweetest sense of refuge, and the most precious treasures. Somehow, in the pouring out, we are filled. It's the mystery of God's math.

> *For the Lord will comfort Zion,*
> *He will comfort all her waste places;*
> *He will make her wilderness like Eden,*
> *And her desert like the garden of the Lord;*
> *Joy and gladness will be found in it,*
> *Thanksgiving and the voice of melody.*
> *– Isaiah 51:3*

I am thankful … that I have been comforted by the Lord.

I am thankful … that His grace is sufficient.

I am thankful … that my wilderness has become like Eden, my desert like the garden of the Lord.

I am thankful … that joy has been restored, that morning has come.

I am thankful … for every moment I watched Faith and Grace and Thomas on the ultrasound screen.

I am thankful … for every hiccup, every movement, every kick, every stretching pain, (not-so-much the nausea and vomiting).

I am thankful … for every dream that we shared together for their lives.

I am thankful … for every conversation that held their names … and for all the times their names have yet to be spoken or written.

I am thankful … that I was chosen to be their mother … for the blessing and privilege of that amazing gift.

I am thankful … that all of my children, in heaven and earth, have their daddy's dark eyes and cute nose.

I am thankful … sweet babies, for prayers prayed over you, songs sung to you, tears wept for you, and the love that spills from the hearts that loved you … and continue to love you.

I am thankful … that Thomas opened his eyes to look up at me and a picture captured that moment of bliss.

I am thankful … that my babies lived on Earth … and that they live in heaven.

I am thankful … Faith, Grace, and Thomas … that I carried you in my womb, held you in my arms, and forever hold you in my heart.

I am thankful … for the promise that I will hold my babies once more in heaven's glory and we will never say good-bye again.

I am thankful … that because our babies lived, many families are comforted in the midst of their sorrow.

I am thankful … that our mourning has been turned into dancing … that our love has sustained the storms of grief … that our God is able to carry us through this life and keep us together as we walk with Him.

I am thankful … that God has blessed me with the boys who remain here with us, filling our house with boisterous noise and the husband who continues to make me laugh, and fills my heart with songs of joy.

You have turned for me my mourning into dancing;
You have put off my sackcloth and clothed me with gladness,
To the end that my glory may sing praise to You and not be silent.
O Lord my God, I will give thanks to You forever.
— Psalm 30:11-12

From The Sufficient Grace Blog: November 14, 2008

Because He Came ...

In a quiet church, almost fifteen years ago, two young kids made a promise to love, honor, and obey. Like two sparrows in a hurricane, they held hands, shaking under the weight of the promise and unaware of what would be required of them.
And He Came ...

Weeping on the floor of their one bedroom apartment ... overwhelmed with the loneliness of a little girl lost and the consuming responsibility of being a wife and mother, she cried out to Him.
And He came ...

On the first silent snowfall, on a cold November day, they held each other and wondered how they were supposed to say good-bye. Forever changed, robbed of the invincibility of youth, robbed of a lifetime of dreams and moments, and all the blessings two little girls would bring.
And He came ...

They stood in the hallway of the hospital as her tears fell in unison with the raindrops trickling down the window pane. How could this be? How can they walk this journey once more, knowing it will end not with the joyous sound of a newborn cry, but instead with the heart wrenching emptiness of another good-bye? Presented with a hopeless outcome, an impossible choice, and the mocking question ... "Where is your God now?" They drove home in the storm.
And He came ...

She prayed and searched day and night for the answers, the evidence that He hadn't turned His back on His two sparrows, leaving them to the merciless destruction of the hurricane. She wept from the unspeakable depths of a mother's heart. Fumbling around in the darkness, she searched for Him. Every step was taken blindly, surrounded by fog so thick, she couldn't tell if her next step would be the one to send her over the edge of the cliff. Would He catch them if they fell?
And He came …

Another silent birth on a warm day in July, they met their fourth child … their second son. They said hello and good-bye.
And He came …

Storms of rage and regret, disappointment and grief, rolled in as the clouds of darkness and doubt, bitterness and pain surrounded them. When the winds of the hurricane threatened fierce and certain destruction, one sparrow flew away and the other remained with broken wings to face the storm.
And He came …

Baby number five … For a moment there was silence, and her heart sank. And then … there it was … life's most precious, miraculous, beautiful sound … the cry of new life … the cry of their baby. They held him and cried in complete awe and gratefulness for the gift of this life.
And He came …

She watched helplessly as her mother painfully and slowly slipped away. As she reassured with promises from His word, they repeated together … He will carry me, He will carry me … and in the depths of her heart, she wondered where He was, and if He would really come.

And He came …

Because He came …

The two sparrows were not alone when they made their commitment to love and cherish each other for all of their days.

Because He came …

She stood up from the floor of their one bedroom apartment, He lifted her head and wiped her tears and gave her courage to begin a new journey.

Because He came …

There was peace in the silent snowfall, beauty in the brokenness, and the hope of the most amazing reunion filled with the unending joys of two little girls who have never known pain, sorrow, regret, sickness, or tears.

Because He came …

There is an answer to the question, "Where is your God now?" There is complete confidence in the sufficient grace of our loving Savior, comfort in the arms of the Comforter, hope in the promise that we will never be forsaken. That His arms are always faithful to carry us. There was strength for the journey. When darkness should have smothered her, joy overcame her at the meeting of her boy … the boy she would only hold for a little while, and yet carry for a lifetime. She felt Him brush past her, and it was almost as if she could just reach out and touch the hem of His garment. Never did she feel His closeness so much, as when He whispered past her to take her sweet boy home. She sang songs of peace and praise as he left her arms. And because He came, one more precious little one will join the forever reunion, with their forever family, in their forever home.

Because He came ...
The sparrow flew home, and the other sparrow's broken wings were mended. They learned to hold on tight, so that when the hurricane winds blow, they will not be separated ... but held together ... closer still.

Because He came ...
He carried her mother home just like He said He would, and He carries His sparrows still today ... through storms and sunshine, laughter and tears.

More than two thousand years ago, the world ached for salvation, swelled with yearning for deliverance, redemption, restoration ... for a Savior to rescue from sin and death. And He came ... a baby King, born in a lowly stable on a quiet night to a peasant girl and her betrothed ... a carpenter. He was in the still, small voice when He whispered past Elijah. And He was in the quiet stable birth when He came to rescue us and sent His angels to tell the lowly shepherds the good news.

His name is Jesus ... and He came for me.
His name is Jesus ... and He came for you.

And Because He came ... there is hope for tomorrow and a promise of a joyful, forever reunion. He will wipe away all of the tears and wash away the loss and regret. He will cleanse and forgive and clothe us in robes of white. The empty arms will be filled. The hungry hearts will be fed. Brokenness will be restored. Mourning will be turned to dancing. And sin and death will be no more.

Because He came … He will carry us through this life.

And because He came … He will come again … in all His glory … to take us home.

Resources

Books:

A Gift of Time – Amy Kuebelbeck and Deborah Davis

Empty Arms – Sherokee Isle

Walking With You – booklet by Kelly Gerken

Walking With You for Fathers – booklet by Kelly Gerken

Waiting With Gabriel – Amy Kuebelbeck

I Will Carry You – Angie Smith

In Faithfulness, He Afflicted Me - Lynette Kraft

I'll Hold You in Heaven – Jack Hayford

Mommy, Please Don't Cry – Linda Deymaz

Heaven is for Real – Todd Burpo

Heaven is for Real for Kids – Todd Burpo

Someday Heaven – Larry Libby

Websites:

Sufficient Grace Ministries has information for families facing a fatal or life-limiting diagnosis in pregnancy, and for those who have experienced the loss of a baby or child. Our Walking With You link offers supportive articles on grief and the loss of a baby. The Dreams of You Shop has a full selection of memory-making items, including the Dreams of You Memory Book and Comfort Bear, available exclusively through Sufficient Grace Ministries. We have a Dreams of You miscarriage book, as well, for families experiencing loss prior to 20 weeks gestation. There are booklets to help families walk through loss, a booklet for fathers, baby gowns made to fit babies in any trimester, special memorial jewelry, and more. Our perinatal hospice links have information on planning for the birth of a baby whose life is expected to be brief. SGM offers support staff and photographers to walk with families in need available 24 hours a day in some parts of the United States. You can find more information or place a request for Dreams of You items at: www.sufficientgraceministries.org

Other sites:

www.perinatalhospice.org
www.benotafraid.net
www.stillstandingmag.com
www.stillbirthday.com
www.babiesremembered.org

Please take the time to check out these resources. I know it can be hard and sometimes we think in our pain that we may not want these things. But, truly it is a time that we cannot get back. There are so many things that I regret not doing and photographs especially that I wish that I had. We would be glad to send you a *Dreams of You Memory Book* and other materials you may need to help prepare for meeting your baby, so please just email us if you have a need: sufficientgraceministries@ gmail.com.

You can also write to us at:

Sufficient Grace Ministries
P.O. Box 243
Deshler, Ohio 43516